Our Gift to You

Thank you for purchasing this book and supporting the work of the Prosperity Economics Movement, which is creating meaningful alternatives to the myths, costs, guesswork, and risks of "typical" financial planning. As our thank-you, we're giving you a FREE 16-page special report:

Permission to Spend: How To Spend Your Principle,
Save a Fortune on Taxes, Increase Your Cash Flow...
and Never Run Out of Money!

Get your free copy at ProsperityPeaks.com/Permission.

Also by Kim D. H. Butler:

Live Your Life Insurance: An Age-Old Approach Revitalized

(Available on Amazon, or get the digital and audio versions at ProsperityPeaks.com)

Busting the Financial Planning Lies: Learn to Use Prosperity Economics to Build Sustainable Wealth

(Available on Amazon.com, or get the bundled version at ProsperityPeaks.com)

Permission to Spend: How To Spend Your Principle, Save a Fortune on Taxes, Increase Your Cash Flow... and Never Run Out of Money!

(A 16-page special report, available as a free download at ProsperityPeaks.com/ Permission)

Look for these forthcoming books from Kim Butler and Prosperity Economics Movement:

Busting the Interest Rate Lies

Busting the Mutual Fund Lies

Busting the Life Insurance Lies

Praise for *Busting the Retirement Lies*

"The truth has to be told! This is not another product sales pitch disguised as 'information.' Instead, Kim Butler exposes the lies behind the entire concept of retirement and shows an alternative to being used up and removed from service much like the gears of an industrial machine. Be prepared to question every statement she makes, and also the rules you thought we all had to live by."

Todd Strobel
"No BS Money Guy"

"*Busting the Retirement Lies* makes a compelling argument that we've been thinking about aging all wrong... and not just financially speaking. This book was a breath of fresh air that provided much food for thought along with inspiration and great tips to make the rest of our years the best. As the Holy Bible has told us—the world has never been right about anything. The concept of retirement never appeared until 1890. It will never work."

R. Nelson Nash
Author of *Becoming Your Own Banker*
and *Building Your Warehouse of Wealth*

"Kim Butler presents a common-sense solution to planning for and transitioning into retirement. She does this with simple yet motivational planning concepts. Her book is a wake-up call to Americans about the need to increase savings rates and the importance of cash flow (velocity of money). She also highlights the error of what retirement has come to mean and how productive and enjoyable it truly can be. Her book has changed the way I look at my businesses, life, and future retirement."

Erkki M. Peippo, CPA, PFS

"Once I opened *Busting the Retirement Lies*, I was hooked and finished it within a matter of hours! This is an incredibly resourceful book. The 401(k) illustrations are a real eye-opener and make you realize how many hands are in what we think is ours. No point in getting angry, though, because this book is empowering and yet another signal to take action and get back (and keep) what is truly yours!"

Jodi Cabral
Holistic Health Coach

"Ms. Butler provides a compelling argument to reconsider the traditional retirement construct so many of us were advised to follow. Kudos to this outside-the-box approach to retirement planning...."

Michael A. Copley

"This book reveals 'the whole truth' about retirement planning and why so many Americans are setting themselves up for failure. Best yet, it shows how to live a long and prosperous life, regardless of your current income. If more people followed Kim's advice in this book, we'd have fewer people approaching retirement with fear and false hopes. It's a lot to expect that the average person can save enough to not work the final decades of our lives, but Kim reframes the whole discussion to let us ask, why we would even want to do that?"

Todd Langford
Truth Concepts Software for advisors and investors

"Kim Butler has a way of challenging the status quo that allows us to see new alternatives to the dilemmas of retirement. *Busting the Retirement Lies* is a must-read for anyone who wants a higher quality of life, and especially those following 'typical' financial strategies (or simply panicking because they are not even doing that.) The examples in the book are tremendous, both the positive and inspirational role models, and the hypothetical (but too common) examples of how fees and taxes will erode most of what people think is 'their' retirement savings. And even when the truth hurts a bit, she leaves her readers with hope, along with specific strategies for a better, more prosperous life."

Kate Phillips
Total Wealth Coaching

REVISED AND EXPANDED THIRD EDITION

Busting the Retirement Lies

Living with Passion, Purpose, and Abundance Throughout Our Lives

KIM D. H. BUTLER

with

Mona Kuljurgis

PROSPERITY ECONOMICS MOVEMENT

Busting the Retirement Lies
Copyright © 2014 Kim D. H. Butler

ISBN: 978-0-9913054-0-7

Third Print Edition
June 2014

Produced in the United States of America

Prosperity Economics Movement
22790 Highway 259 South
Mount Enterprise, TX 75681
www.ProsperityPeaks.com

Contents

Foreword ix

Preface... xi

Introduction xv

Chapter 1: Getting Older, Getting Better 1

Chapter 2: Match Your Purpose with Your Prowess.................... 13

Chapter 3: Find Work You Love... 21

Chapter 4: Strategize How to Keep Doing Meaningful Work 29

Chapter 5: Save 20 Percent of Your Income................................ 39

Chapter 6: The Reality of Retirement Plans................................ 65

Chapter 7: Live and Share with Passion 97

Conclusion 107

Resources... 111

Notes 115

About the Author 119

About Prosperity Economics Movement...................................... 121

Further Information... 125

Foreword

In the early '90s, I helped my company downsize (or as the company euphemistically called it, "right size") for the first time in their ninety-year history. My job as the Human Resource Manager was to call in about 70 of my co-workers and offer to move them into retirement and to offer them a generous severance package to voluntarily leave their employment. My company, unlike many companies today, had a pension plan as well as a defined contribution 401(k) option.

With each individual interview, I was amazed at how each employee thought of, and in fact, defined the word "retirement." Most were totally unprepared for the eventuality that faces all employees—the end of their employment. Those who had thought of and planned for that day, were prepared and ready to go. For the vast majority, however, the stark reality of the end of their jobs was a major jolt. I am still haunted to this day by the looks of disbelief, horror, and fear; their drained faces firmly gripped them as they suddenly realized their lives were about to change, and in ways they could not possibly have imagined. After several interviews, I began looking specifically at the pension balances and discovered that, on average, those hard-working, dedicated employees (many of whom had known no other jobs) would be retiring on 26 percent of their current incomes. And since I was familiar with many of their financial situations, I knew they would be retiring on 26 percent of what *they couldn't live on the month before*. Needless to say, this experience had a profound impact on those unsuspecting souls. My perspective was changed forever as well, as I pondered the meaning of retirement for them and in my own life.

Kim's new book is a welcome and desperately needed look into the realities of life after employment, one that will help take the blinders off people who have unknowingly and unsuspectedly bought into the lies of the mythical world of retirement. This is a mindset fully entrenched in the scarcity mentality of the central planners of a hundred years ago—these planners firmly believed that, because of the limited number of jobs that can exist in an economy, older workers must leave their jobs to make room for younger workers to take their place. Thankfully, this mindset is obsolete and the time has come for a massive shift in perspective. I am excited to see Kim's *Busting the Retirement Lies* help make this happen.

Jim Kindred, Founder
Financial Strategies Group, LLC

Preface

Running out of money ranks as the greatest fear for many Americans over age 50 today. Study after study shows that most of us are not saving enough. But "enough" for what? Enough for what has become the universal goal of life in recent decades—the goal to stop working at some arbitrary "age of retirement." Absurdly, we've set a cultural standard that many of us will never successfully reach. Sure, many will stop working, even before 70, but can they afford to do so? Our over-taxed social services and Medicaid programs suggest not. And perhaps a better question is, "Why should we want to stop working?"

I have worked in the financial services industry for over 25 years, but I consider myself in the business of helping people *holistically*— not the business of teaching clients to simply accumulate bigger piles of money. (My firm doesn't even manage assets, and we teach our clients to control their own assets and focus on cash flow rather than accumulation.) We practice what we call "Prosperity Economics" rather than "financial planning," because we believe that prosperity is about so much more than money. We are not just financial beings; we are human beings. And how we approach aging—culturally, mentally, physically, spiritually, and financially—affects the quality of life we will enjoy, for years to come.

Prosperity Economics doesn't aim to help people succeed better at prevailing flawed strategies; rather, it offers a total paradigm shift. It questions typical financial assumptions and advice that many have come to accept as true, and instead it promotes the strategies, principles, and practices used by the wealthy for many decades, even centuries. Prosperity Economics offers not only a different destination than traditional financial planning—we like to think of it as "Prosperity Peaks" as opposed to the proverbial "house on the hill"—but also better pathways up the mountainside to these Prosperity Peaks.

It's important to point out that I say Prosperity Peaks—plural, instead of singular—because I believe there is no one single "Peak" for any person. Instead, I believe there are many Peaks for each of us and that most folks should seek many summits throughout their lives: many different retirements, times of travel, periods of enlightenment, spiritual pathways, and anything else that qualifies as a Prosperity Peak experience for them.

At TheNextHill.com, blogger MelP writes:

> ... *no one is ever really over the hill. Sometimes we reach the top of one hill and have to find another one. Sometimes in mid-climb we recognize a mistake and decide to start over. Sometimes our hill collapses, and we just have to move on. But we are never, ever, over the hill. There is always another one to climb.*

Life is long. And it's winding. There is time to scale many peaks, and even cherish the valleys in between, for all of us.

I invite you to learn more about the Prosperity Economics

Movement at the end of this book, and explore the Prosperity Economics alternative strategies in this book and others, available at ProsperityPeaks.com, where you'll find information and education to help you see the full picture of your finances and reach the many Peaks available to us all.

As we learn together, we all benefit, breaking the grip of the corporate financial industry on our dollars and our minds, and create more prosperity for all of us.

May you always relish the view from high upon the Prosperity Peaks.

Kim Butler, Founder
Prosperity Economics Movement

INTRODUCTION

**"Retirement is not in my vocabulary.
They aren't going to get rid of me that way."**

~Betty White

Retirement Lies

It's no surprise that the concept of retirement is nowhere to be found in ancient times or in ancient texts, including the Bible. In the Middle Ages, when people spoke of retiring, they meant either turning in for the night or retreating from the battlefront.

The word's usage in the current sense—"withdrawal from one's position or occupation or from active working life"—is traced to the year 1590. But the term or concept came into popular usage less than a hundred years ago, with the passing of the 1935 Social Security Act. And the word "retiree" is an Americanism that only came into use in the 1940s!

The Retirement Lies that permeate our American culture and beyond have taken root like a pack of weeds that obscure the garden that was previously in their place. In less than a century, they have come to be accepted as "the way things are," or at the very least, "the way things should be." Perhaps the biggest Lie is the very concept of retirement itself, which I believe is an inherently flawed idea. And this big Lie is supported by a host of other Lies upon which it is built. These Lies tell us:

The reward of work is the cessation of work. We should work (typically full-time, nearly every week of the year) until age 65, or some other arbitrarily determined age. After a lifetime of work, we earn the right to "retire" from work completely.

Retirement is good for us. No more alarms, no more commuting, no deadlines, no more work! Nothing but leisure. Just sit back, relax, and enjoy "the good life."

Our retirement accounts will ensure we never have work again. Our 401(k)s, IRAs, and similar qualified funds are designed to maximize, protect, grow, and preserve our money. If we simply put a portion of our earnings into our retirement accounts, those investments will provide for us in the decades beyond retirement, even to age 100 or beyond. (I could go on and on about the financial lies, but instead I'll suggest my other and forthcoming "Busting Lies" books about Financial Planning, Interest Rates, Insurance, and Mutual Funds.)

Older people are not as productive, valuable, or creative. At some point, typically between 64 and 70, it's time for us to move aside and let the younger workforce take over our jobs. Elderly people are of limited use to society.

And the list could continue....

In my view, the almost universally applied model of quitting a job or career entirely at a certain age has never really worked for most people, cannot work, and—if I had my way—*should not* work for most people today.

Why do I say this? Three main reasons:

1. **I believe human beings were put on earth to serve.** We serve our families, then our communities, and more and more in this globally connected age, the world. The very

intent of retirement—when defined as "to take out of service" or "withdrawal from one's position or from active working life"— doesn't sound like fun at all. When we stop serving and live a life that is focused on self, our lives can go downhill in a hurry. Yes, the media has put forth the idea of one's golden years filled with golf and fishing, art and food, and plenty of travel. But I have it on good authority that leisure and inertia have limited capacity to create a fulfilling and satisfying life.

2. **Can we afford to retire?** In our 20+ years in financial services, I've seen that most folks cannot financially afford to retire *and* maintain their accustomed standard of living. Some families do build enough wealth during their working years to live off the rest of their lives. But for most of us, the idea of saving money from age 30 to 65 and then living off that money from age 65 to age 100—yes, age 100!—borders on the impossible. And *where* we save our money erodes its growth. We underestimate the impact of inflation and taxation, and most importantly, Americans simply don't save enough.

3. **Retirement isn't good for your health.** Last but not least, from my experience with people who have retired, and those who have not, I've learned that retirement just isn't good for you—physically, emotionally, psychologically, or spiritually. While the jury is still out on that subject, numerous studies have shown that an abrupt shift from full-time work to retirement can have negative impacts on our health.

My father can attest to that. My father became a school teacher right out of college and eventually worked his way up to school principal, a position he held until age 58. For a variety of reasons, including my mother's early passing, he retired. Living on the same 40-acre farm he had for many years, there were numerous tasks to keep him physically occupied, and he was very involved in his church. Yet, over time, he felt emotionally disconnected from the young people he was used to serving. He volunteered in some classrooms and mentored a few student teachers, but there was still something missing. Then, at 69 years old, he was asked by a local country charter school to advise them as they worked through some issues. This led to a part-time job as their principal. Today, while he's only supposed to put in 30 hours a week, he usually puts in 40+ hours because of the joy and energy he gets from serving again.

Much more than a "financial book," *Busting the Retirement Lies* is about busting the lies of retirement in all their forms. For some, retiring at 65 or even 75 is a financial improbability, and the mere idea of retirement is a set-up for frustration, failed expectations, and financial struggle. For others who do build nest eggs ample to handle any challenge of longevity, health, or inflation, retirement challenges us to find purpose and passion without the structure that work can bring. For all, retirement can be the false gold at the end of the proverbial rainbow that limits our wealth while robbing us of the meaning that lifelong contribution (paid or voluntary) can give our lives.

So, if I'm suggesting that you shouldn't retire, what *should* you do instead?

Do What You Love, Live Long, and Prosper

Busting the Retirement Lies presents a number of steps that will help you look forward to another productive and satisfying epoch in your life.

Getting better, not just older... to 100 years or beyond! Science is beginning to learn that our lifespans are largely self-limited due to our ways of living. As medicine and technology discover more about how we can improve our lifestyles for longevity, we can make better choices. More people are living past the 100-year mark now than ever before—and more will be doing so with each passing year.

Match your purpose with your prowess. In other words, figure out what you're good at and what your innate calling or "soul purpose" is. There are several ways to do this, and I will propose a few that I find particularly helpful.

Find work or volunteer opportunities you love. Based on what you learn and know about yourself, make lists of services you could provide and start doing them right away. Some will earn money, and some won't, but there are many opportunities out there, and I'll share some ideas that will get you thinking.

Strategize how to keep doing meaningful work, both paid and unpaid, for the rest of your life. Doing work you love also has a financial component, especially if that work is unpaid, so I've devoted a large portion of this book to financial matters—specifically, saving for retirement.

Save 20 percent of your income. This advice goes back to biblical ages! Save generously, and then use a portion of your savings throughout your life for sabbaticals, long vacations, and times when work doesn't earn the money you'd like.

Learn the reality of retirement plans. I break down the facets of the most prevalent retirement plan, the 401(k), and factor in every variable to show you the whole truth about your money.

Live and share with passion. Human beings were built to push our limits a bit, so consider pushing yourself at least once each week to stay engaged in life. Plus, take special note of those things that energize you and bring you enthusiasm, whether big or small, and incorporate them more into your life, and encourage those around you to do the same. Life is a work in progress, so keep stretching past your comfort zone and ticking off items on a well-thought-out bucket list.

The first chapters of the book examine our current realities and cultural assumptions about aging and retirement, while offering principles that challenge conventional thinking. I personally use these principles, many of them modeled by my own role models and mentors, as guideposts in my own life.

But the Retirement Lies aren't just conceptual—they are numerical as well, permeating our financial institutions as well as our culturally conditioned beliefs about money. In chapters five and six of this book, I crunch some serious retirement-planning numbers. To do this, I utilize graphs, charts, and calculators provided by Truth Concepts software. Truth Concepts helps financial advisors demystify the math of their clients' financial lives so that they can understand the whole truth about their money. Designed for financial professionals but available to anyone, this valued tool is available at TruthConcepts.com.

Throughout the book, I present examples and case studies of individuals who have chosen a non-traditional "retirement" route in the form of Retirement Profiles. These stories give flesh to the concepts of the book by providing concrete illustrations of what the principles look like in real life.

This book and others published by the Prosperity Economics Movement (you can find them at ProsperityPeaks.com) exist to help you make your life richer in every moment. It is our aim to bust not only the lies of disenfranchisement, marginalization, and inertia in older age, but also the lies of a financial industry that too often does not have our best interest at heart. I sincerely hope you use this book to face the youth-obsessed, commercially driven cultural biases head on—to live, both financially and otherwise, rich, valuable, contributive lives well into retirement and beyond.

As Sophia Loren once said, "There is a fountain of youth: it is your mind, your talents, the creativity you bring to your life and the lives of people you love. When you learn to tap this source, you will truly have defeated age."

GETTING OLDER,
GETTING BETTER

"Getting older is inevitable. Aging is optional."

—*Mario Martinez*

Ageism in America

Renowned women's health advocate, author, speaker, and medical doctor Christiane Northrup advises people to never state their age. She encourages those faced with the question to respond, "My age is none of my business," or "I am ageless and timeless."

It's an odd piece of advice coming from a progressive researcher writing on cutting-edge health practice and theory from a country that boasts having overcome so many stereotypes.

But, there is a reason behind Northrup's seemingly throwback position.

Citing the work of Mario Martinez, neuropsychologist and founder of the Biocognitive Science Institute, Northrup implores people not to state their age because of what Martinez calls "cultural portals." Cultural portals are preconceived notions engrained in society and linked to certain milestones in life. These portals influence the way people are viewed in the culture and, consequently, how they are treated by others. And how people are treated in a society inevitably influences how they, themselves, feel and behave.

A cultural portal may include many stereotypes: rebelling against authority in your teens, becoming sexually promiscuous if you are male, embracing parenthood in early adulthood, and deterioration and decline in older age.

Northrup and Martinez believe that your health and well-being are directly related to the cultural expectations placed upon you. Thus, if the culture's expectation is to become obsolete and irrelevant in older age, that belief directly impacts your physiology, your psychology, and the perceptions you maintain about yourself.

The researchers draw a contrast between what they call biologic age and chronologic age—chronologic being the date-related age reflected on your driver's license, biologic age being the age at which your body actually functions. Biologic age—to your benefit or your detriment—can vary considerably from chronologic age—and biologic age is coauthored by the prevailing expectations and stereotypes of the culture.

Though Martinez's and Northrup's work is cutting edge today, it is certainly not new. In 1875, Mary Baker Eddy wrote in *Science and Health with Key to the Scriptures*:

> *Never record ages. Chronological data are no part of the vast forever. Time-tables of birth and death are so many conspiracies against manhood and womanhood. Except for the error of measuring and limiting all that is good and beautiful, man would enjoy more than threescore years and ten and still maintain his vigor, freshness, and promise.*[1]

Wicked Hostility

It is difficult, however, to maintain vigor, freshness, and promise when cultural cues regarding aging are so negative. Rather than being seen as a worthwhile, experienced, and discerning stage of life, aging is often viewed as a deteriorating and worthless passage, mostly due to the American single-minded obsession with outward appearance. The most pervasive, insidious, and overlooked form of discrimination in America today is ageism.

With a modern-day culture relentlessly controlled by commercial media and obsessed with image, current societal norms exhibit an acid disdain for those who do not conform to media ideals. As these ideals mostly exclude anyone over 40, a rampant, insidious contempt pervades our culture with what author and social critic Margaret Morganroth Gullette calls a "wicked hostility" toward the elderly.[2]

It is important to remember, however, that this hostility achieves a very deliberate goal. The corporate media successfully controls and manipulates younger people by tightening its vice grip on societal norms. In doing so, it replaces the role of the elder in society, ensuring the voice of reason, experience, and discernment is not brought to the table.

Although the engine of the media is powerful, some responsibility does belong to seniors themselves. Cohousing advocate and blogger Chuck Durrett believes that, perhaps due to the *influence* of popular media, older Americans have renounced their role as elders in society. He feels seniors must *earn* the respect they once held and wish to command:

> *Being an elder once meant earning respect by playing an active role in teaching younger generations, a role that's seldom fulfilled today... seniors earn elderhood by helping younger generations understand how to be accountable.*[3]

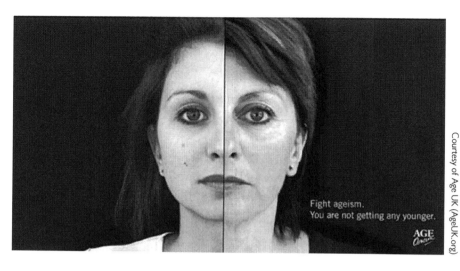

Not for Nothing

None of this is to say that as you approach, achieve, and pass beyond retirement age it's time to hang up your hat and throw in the towel. It's only to get the full picture of the cultural landscape you will be facing—prejudices, discrimination, and all.

Regardless of perceptions and discrimination, human beings were meant to serve, and there's no one better to contribute to the culture as a whole than those with discernment, experience, and care.

One woman who embodies these attributes is Louise Hay, founder and CEO of the largest spirituality and self-help publishing house in the world, Hay House Publishing. As of this writing, Ms. Hay approaches her 87th birthday and sent out this message to her email list:

> *I'm going to be 87 next week. I choose to see my life moving in different directions, all of them equally good. Some things are even better now than the way they were in my youth.*
>
> *My younger years were filled with fear. My todays are filled with confidence.*

My own life really didn't begin to have meaning until I was in my mid-40s. At the age of 50, I began my writing career on a very small scale. The first year I made a profit of $42.

At 55, I ventured into the world of computers. They scared me. But I took classes and overcame the fear. Today, I have three computers and travel with my iPad and iPhone everywhere. At 60, I had my first garden. At this same time, I enrolled in a children's art class and began to paint. At 70 and 80 I was more creative, and my life continues to get richer and richer in every moment.

Longevity and Income—the Crucial Link

According to a University of Washington study for the Institute of Health Metrics and Evaluation, American men in 2010 could expect to live 76.1 years—almost six years more than in 1985. American women could expect to live 80.8 years—three years more than in 1985.[4]

Good news. It's the direction we'd like to be going. But, here's the kicker:

The observed increase in longevity and life expectancy is directly correlated with income.

It is an uncomfortable and inconvenient truth that Americans' lifespans are associated with their financial resources at retirement. Those thick-maned, silver-haired actors biking and cruising the Mediterranean in TV ads represent only a segment of retirees; others' lives look quite different.

> "Retirement kills more people than hard work ever did."
> ~Malcolm Forbes

In data pulled from the study and featured in a 2013 *Washington Post* article, a women's life expectancy in the wealthy coastal area of St. John's County, Florida is 83 years; for men, it is 78 years. But in neighboring inland Putnam county, where income and housing values are half those of St. John's, women's life expectancy is 78 years and men's 71—a five- and seven-year difference in longevity in counties only a few minutes' drive apart. And this pattern is repeated throughout every region of the country.[5] You can explore health trends in your region by viewing the amazing interactive U.S. Health Map at HealthMetricsAndEvaluation.org.

It is not my intent, by the way, to scare you into paralysis or paint the most dire picture of life's later years. In fact, I aim to do the opposite. These data represent statistical averages, and every life story is different. It is my hope that studies like these spur you to action, especially financially wise actions such as earning, saving, and investing. Along with your innate calling, financial resources do make a difference, in the length of your life and in its quality.

Centenarians and Beyond

Despite an often-daunting picture, it is still important to remember that, even though there are differences in the rates of life expectancy increases, longevity on the whole is on the rise. Life expectancy for both rich and poor is increasing across the board.

In fact, there are more than half a million centenarians in the world today, and that number is only expected to increase. The United Kingdom's Office of National Statistics has forecasted that 35 percent of its country's residents born in 2012 will live to be 100 or more.

According to educator, author, and entrepreneur Steve Franklin, research suggests that centenarians have been doubling in number every decade since the 1950s. "By 2050," Franklin contends, "there will be close to 1,000,000 American centenarians." Franklin is founder of The Centenarian Project (100Wisdom.com), which captures the "authentic wisdom from America's centenarians."

When we start thinking about our lives in terms of 100-plus years, many things take on a whole new meaning. For example, if you have a long-term project, knowing that you may have many more years on earth helps you tackle it in a patient way. Not feeling like you have to get it done this weekend enables you to enjoy the process more, smell the roses (and feel the thorns) along the way, and do a better job by taking the time to do it right. In our "fast-food society," we expect things overnight when a 20- or 30-year perspective might help us to not only enjoy the journey, but also feel better about the results along the way.

In fact, according to Dr. Henry Lodge in his book *Younger Next Year*, "It turns out that 70 percent of American aging is not real aging. It's just decay. It's rot from the stuff that we do. All the lifestyle diseases... diabetes, obesity, heart disease, Alzheimer's, cancers, etc.... those are all decay. Nature doesn't have that in store for any of us. We go and buy it off the rack."

The Wisdom of the Ages

So, how does a person live to 100 (or beyond) and love it? In *Celebrate 100: Centenarian Secrets to Success in Business and Life*, Franklin and Lynn Peters Adler distill advice from more than 500 centenarians into seven secrets for living a long and prosperous life. An inspiring group of active men and women, they are a diverse group of entrepreneurs, athletes, philanthropists, and hobbyists who affirm that age is merely a number. And while one of the secrets to longevity is having good genes (some have relatives in their family tree who lived long lives, though many do not), the other six secrets are habits that anyone can cultivate:

Maintaining a Positive Attitude—Almost all of the centenarians interviewed identified themselves as optimistic people and recommended a positive yet realistic attitude as important throughout one's life.

Eating in Moderation—While some had become vegetarians, only 20 percent said they had ever been on a specialized diet plan. The one thing the majority of centenarians agreed on was portion size and eating *quality* food, not quantities of it.

Staying Active—"Move it or lose it," says Louise Caulder, age 101. "I don't leave my bedroom before doing 30 minutes of stretches. Later, I walk a mile. Three times a week I play bridge. You've got to exercise your mind as well as your body—everyone knows that, but I wonder how many are actually doing it." Centenarians seemed more likely to actually be doing it, with some even taking home medals in the Senior Games.

Keeping the Faith—Nearly all centenarians surveyed said their faith has sustained them. Most believe they have lived so long to fulfill whatever purpose God has for them. "Perhaps we are here to be an example to others in hard times," says Roberta McRaney, 101, who had two homes (the original and the rebuilt home) struck by lightning and burn to the ground.

Clean Living—"Just stay out of trouble," says Harry Alder, 101. While the definition of *clean living* varied, many centenarians said it means "doing what you know is right and following your conscience." Also, 75 percent of the people surveyed had never smoked, whole most of the rest had stopped decades earlier. And while some never drank, most enjoyed an occasional cocktail or a glass of wine.

A Loving Family—Their loved ones and relatives were universally important to centenarians. They enjoyed their roles as family elders and derived much pleasure from watching younger generations come into their own.

As Adler asserts in a Forbes.com article, "Despite the inevitable ups and downs, the biggest secret these centenarians shared is that living to 100 is worth the effort. Like climbing a mountain, we should aspire to reach that height, not just because it is there, but because the view from the top is unsurpassed."

MATCH YOUR PURPOSE WITH YOUR PROWESS

"At an early age, you started hearing it: It's a virtue to be 'well-rounded.' ... They might as well have said: Become as dull as you possibly can be."

—Donald O. Clifton in his book Living Your Strengths: Discover Your God-Given Talents and Inspire Your Community

Each of us has an innate calling that drives us forward and leads us to a happier, more fulfilling life. In the rushed world of work and family, perhaps just a few of us know what that calling is. Some of us may have forgotten it over time, and some of us have yet to discover it.

Not all of us have had a chance to explore what we'd love to do in the world, particularly if adult responsibilities kicked in early in life. However, retirement isn't just about savings plans and tax deferrals; it is a time, if planned for properly, to investigate all the different areas of life we didn't get a chance to explore when our time was preoccupied with scratchin' for a dollar.

Our innate calling, when combined with the skills we've developed and nurtured over time—or even those skills we may have put aside and forgotten—gives us the basis to live productive, joyful, and satisfying lives.

One of the best tools I've found to help live that life is The Kolbe System™ (Kolbe.com). Created by Kathy Kolbe, it helps you identify a successful balance between your innate calling, what you like to do, and where your skills and capabilities actually lie. I was introduced to Kolbe's insightful life's work in the mid-1990s via Dan Sullivan, founder of The Strategic Coach® Program. Even though the Kolbe offices were right down the street from me, and an internationally known company at that, I was unaware of the impact the system would have on my life. Kolbe originally focused on techniques that helped students navigate the educational process, but now helps adults visualize and realize their passions—both in organizations and as individuals.

One of Kathy Kolbe's maxims, "Success is the freedom to be yourself," is a guiding principle of her work; yet knowing yourself is one of the hardest things to do. I strongly encourage you to visit Kolbe.com and spend the $50 and 20 minutes to take the Kolbe A™ Index. (Kolbe Y™ is available for people under age 18, for only $10.)

Giving you specifics on how *you* work to get results will help you know whether you are seeking out the right opportunity, be it paid employment or as a volunteer. With the Kolbe A Index, your search for your innate calling and the opportunities to express that calling will be easier because, when you are doing work you love, it no longer feels like work.

Another tool I've found helpful is Donald O. Clifton's website StrengthsFinder.com. Known as "the father of strengths-based psychology," Clifton created his Strengths Finder assessment is based on 34 "themes" or strengths that identify five main inclinations or propensities, on the premise that building on strengths is much easier than trying to improve weaknesses.

Using these two tools helped me identify the specific areas of my profession that most closely align with my strengths, and how those strengths get me results. For example, one thing important to me is a sense of achievement. Knowing this helped me realize why, even on a Saturday, I need to feel like I've *accomplished something*. However, because I'm an adherent of Dan Sullivan's Strategic Coach® program and his "Free Day®" concept, something we'll visit in chapter 4, I like to keep my Saturdays free from business. So, through trial and error, I found a few things to do that are not business related, yet give me a sense of accomplishment. For example, because I live on a farm, in the summer I spend many hours mowing pastures and doing farm work, while in the winter I crochet the alpaca fiber my animals produce.

Retirement Profile: Jeanne Robertson (1945–)
Keynote Speaker and Humorist
"Loving Life—and Laughing at It, Too!"

Jeanne Robertson has been making a living looking at the lighter side of life for nearly 50 years. Now in her late 60s, Robertson shows no signs of stopping. Her career travelling around the country as a popular speaker is in full swing. In fact, she has recently added a whole new dimension after a YouTube video of one of her presentations went viral.

The six-foot-two 1963 Miss North Carolina figured she had a knack for public speaking while delivering over 500 speeches the year after winning her title. (She also went on to win Miss Congeniality in the Miss America pageant later that year.)

According to *The Burlington Times-News*, in a September 6, 2009 article, "While other people her age may be thinking about retirement, for Robertson that is not an option right now. She said the Internet has opened up a world of opportunities she never expected, so as long as she can deliver and as 'long as the lights are down low to look pretty good out there,' she will be on stage. 'It's a whole new world,' she added, 'and I am embracing it.'"

In addition to her live speeches and performances, Robertson makes extensive use of online media through marketing short, downloadable clips on iTunes. She's learned how to title her stories so they are downloaded more and has partnered with Sirius XM radio, which plays her stories several times each day on the Family Comedy Channel.

Robertson's secret to keeping her material fresh is keeping a journal. According to the Times-News article, "Everything that happens in my life that is funny goes into the journal… Though not everything that happens in life is funny, if you look hard, you will find that a lot of it is…. In the 1960s, I was talking about beauty pageants…. Now, I am talking about getting older."

Retirement Profile: W. Edwards Deming (1900–1993) Management Consultant
"A Passion for Quality—a Life Lesson from a Business Philosopher"

The founding "guru" of systems thinking and quality management, the unassuming W. Edwards Deming from Laramie, Wyoming turned around the fortunes of the Ford Motor Company and a host of post-war Japanese industries. He was still doing management seminars and workshops until just ten days before his passing in December 1993.

Dr. Deming's work in Japan focused on improving product durability and reliability and had a lasting impact on Japan's emergence from post-war destruction and poverty. His name and fame in Japan were second only to that of General Douglas MacArthur, yet he remained little known in the United States until well into the 1970s—as American industry equated better quality with prohibitively higher cost.

Only when Japanese electronics and automobiles began to infiltrate American markets did U.S. industry sit up and take notice. Ford Motor Company was one of the first to seek Deming's counsel; however, their executives were not pleased when Deming told them that their quality problems were due to poor management. But under his patient tutelage, Ford improved its quality standards and eventually turned up the road to success. Companies like Xerox, Dow Chemical, AT&T, and *The New York Times* then also sought out Deming's counsel.

With such a passion for quality, is it surprising then that Deming himself lived a quality life? "Well into his 90s," according to a *New York Times* December 21, 1993 article by Joshua Holusha, "Mr. Deming maintained an active travel schedule, crisscrossing the country to conduct seminars and consult with companies he considered sufficiently motivated to benefit from his attention. He also lectured at Columbia University's Business School and taught continuously at New York University's Stern School of Business from 1946 until the end of the spring term this year."

The story of this inspiring man makes you wonder: What if all of us paid a little more attention to the *quality* of what we do and how we think?

FIND WORK YOU LOVE

"Retirement is the ugliest word in the language."

—*Ernest Hemingway*

Have you ever just lazed around the house all day, thinking that would rejuvenate you?

Did it?

Perhaps, at least for a while, but probably not for long.

Leisure, though sometimes precisely what is needed for certain situations, has a limited ability over the long haul to fulfill our lives. As human beings, we were put on this earth to serve and add value. Knowing ourselves well enough to match our strengths and instinctive way of life to our work can make it so we can't wait to get up every morning.

Simply put, we need to find work we *love*—whether it's full-time, part-time, flex-time, freelance, phased, sabbatical, seasonal, paid, personal, volunteer, or whatever. And there's no better time to find that work than a well-funded retirement.

One resource for matching your work with your passions is Instinctive Life (InstinctiveLife.com). Founder Tammi Brannan's strength is helping others figure out their purpose in life—drilling down to that tiny jewel of motivation, authenticity, and joy that really moves us and makes our lives sing. As I've said, this is a great pursuit at any age, but if retirement is your first chance to lift your head above water and contemplate the notion, Brannan's work is a great place to start.

When we are aware of our purpose and conscious of our strengths, it is much easier to find our calling, paid or volunteer. The process of discovering—or in some cases re-discovering—your "instinctive life," as Brannan puts it, can be a raucous adventure and a spiritual journey, and Brannan offers great tools, techniques, and guidance to move you along the path.

Keep Changing Until You Find What's Right for You

Learning can be exciting, and humans *want* to learn. We are programmed for it. And we are best situated for learning when the topic fits with our life purpose in some way, because this leads to natural curiosity. When we are curious about the subject matter, it's much easier to be excited about the learning required to do that work. This goes full circle—your life purpose leads to topic interest, which leads to curiosity, which leads to excitement, which leads to learning, which is crucial to fulfilling your life purpose. Pursuing this cycle makes us happier people while working, and happier at home and during off hours. Thus, if you view work as something you'll do your entire life, rather than as drudgery to be endured for a few decades, you'll take the time to find the right fit. Thankfully, in today's economy, changing jobs is normal. So, keep changing until you find what's right for you.

Your Talents Are Needed, Even If You Don't Think So

And if another job is not what you want, take a chance and make a list of services you can provide, based on your talents and what you love—and start providing them, now. What you have to offer is needed, even if you don't think so. Offer these services simply because you love doing them or because they bring in a little extra money. In time, they may lead to a full-time business or other opportunity. And because you are operating within an area you enjoy, whatever opportunities come your way are more likely to fit well with your instinctive purpose.

Putting together this list of services can uncover a literal world of possibilities. Thankfully, most everything that needs to be done matches up with people who like to do it. (Yes, there really are people who like mowing the lawn and doing paperwork.)

Keep in mind, your list doesn't have to be income related, especially if you've planned well for retirement.

Another option is to start or join a barter circle, a group of people creatively matching individuals' time and services with needs in their immediate communities. Find others who like to do the things you don't like to do. Barter circles, sometimes called "community time banks," extend between more than two people: Person A performs a service for Person B, who does something for Person C, and so on back to Person A. Check out Useful Services Exchange at RestonUSE.org for ideas. It's a fun way to remain active, stay social, and make a great contribution along the way.

Another example of this concept, though a for-profit business model, is Seniors Helping Seniors. This organization matches demand with supply and helps keep experienced, older adults active and earning money, assisting peers with whom they can relate in a variety of daily tasks and providing basic human companionship. I encourage you to explore SeniorsHelpingSeniors. com, which will give you a better idea of what can be done for others—and, in the bargain, for yourself.

Retirement Profile: Steven R. Covey (1932–2012)
Author, Speaker, Thought Leader on Transformation
"Sharpen That Saw!"

Chances are, you've probably heard of Steven Covey and his timeless bestseller, The *7 Habits of Highly Effective People*. A leader in the field of self-help publishing and coaching, Dr. Covey's work has been transformative for millions—and informed his long and productive career.

Until his unexpected passing at age 79—the result of a bicycle accident in 2012—Covey exemplified the maxims of self-reliance and focus he urged on his readers. His advice and ideas built his multi-million-dollar publishing empire and focused almost exclusively on character and what things each of us can control and influence within ourselves. Not much of what Covey wrote is new or rocket science; most is common sense. But it is common sense that many of us seem to have forgotten or mistakenly think is no longer relevant.

In short, Covey promoted the following "Seven Habits":

1. Be proactive.
2. Begin with the end in mind.
3. Put first things first.
4. Think win-win.
5. Seek first to understand, then to be understood.
6. Synergize.
7. Sharpen the saw

This last of the seven habits is a call to constantly improve oneself—mentally, physically, technically—which is especially important for people as they age.

Though primarily focused on business, Covey's principles apply to virtually every aspect of life—and at any stage. The thought leader certainly practiced what he preached, making an active contribution throughout his life and longer, as his wisdom lives on in his work.

Retirement Profile: Tom Peters (1942–)
Author, Speaker, and Management Consultant
"Still Pursuing Excellence!"

Tom Peters, another leader in personal and professional development, published his seminal work, *In Search of Excellence*, almost a decade before Steven Covey's.

When he neared 70 years old, Peters began contemplating his extraordinarily productive and busy life as a management consultant and motivational expert. Following a health challenge a few years ago, Peters took the opportunity to reflect on the concept of "retirement" and "slowing down." According to a September 1, 2010 *U.S. News & World Report* article, the management guru "has been asking himself the same questions as millions of others who are in or nearing the traditional age of retirement."

Well known for working long, punishing hours and thriving on a schedule that would make others quail, Peters is now seizing the opportunity to reevaluate priorities: "...when you make an enormous transition [in working life], you really have to be careful not to find another way to work 18 hours a day, six days a week doing something else... immediately finding a way to fill your time is really, really bad news."

But his advice is not for retirees only; Peters addresses the change all those in the working world are facing. In his book, *Talent: Develop It, Sell It, Be It*, Peters warns, "The microchip will colonize all rote activities. And we will have to scramble to reinvent ourselves—as we did when we came off the farm and went into the factory, and then as we were ejected from the factory and delivered to the white-collar towers.... The reinvented you and the reinvented me will have no choice but to scramble and add value in some meaningful way."

At the same time, Peters does not believe that reinventing yourself is the answer to everything. "Statistically and emotionally," Peters says, "I believe that the way I can be of help to society is by doing what I know and what I've been good at."

STRATEGIZE HOW TO KEEP DOING MEANINGFUL WORK

**"Retirement at sixty-five is ridiculous.
When I was sixty-five I still had pimples."**

—*George Burns*

Retirement usually takes place at age 65. But where did that number come from?

"Your 65th birthday is nothing more than an arbitrary line scratched across your life by someone else for reasons that have nothing to do with you or your well-being."[6] That's the blunt and pretty accurate view of blogger MelP at TheNextHill.com. He goes on to write: "Historically, retirement has been nothing more than a tool for getting older people out of the way. It is bad for older people, middle-aged workers, and society as a whole. It is time to re-think the whole notion."

I feel strongly that laws protecting forced retirement in the United States need to be changed. I have several clients who have been forced to retire by company rules—rules written long ago when a certain age was believed to come with limitations. It is sad to see people who love their work, and are skilled and experienced at it, asked to leave just because of their age. With life expectancy increasing, and physical and mental health on the rise, there's no reason to stop work if you don't want to.

Experience counts in a variety of ways, and it can be very beneficial for businesses to retain experienced people. If you relate to this scenario, consider staying on at your workplace but talking with your employer about working fewer hours, job-sharing, working from home, or any other option that gives variety to the typical 40-hour workweek. That way, they can keep an experienced person, and you can keep working and enjoy life a bit more—think three-day weekends every week.

When approaching your employer, just be sure to pitch your ideas as a benefit to the company; if you start the conversation only from what is to your benefit, it is less likely to be well received. If you aren't sure how your proposed arrangement could be good for the company, talk with trusted coworkers who might be in a position to offer suggestions—while keeping your plans quiet.

Alternatively, consider quitting your job and taking extended time off with the idea of coming back and consulting for the company on your time schedule. Carmen Langford, who is in her early 70s, did just that as head of microbiology for a hospital in Texas. She now works about three days a week—sometimes less, sometimes more—and focuses only on what she enjoyed the most in her former position. Because she is a paid consultant, she can also take longer vacations or not work at all on any given day if she doesn't want to.

This same dynamic is standard in the movie industry, which has long operated on a freelance basis. Skilled contributors, from directors to actors to stunt women to extras, come together to work on a particular movie then go their separate ways. In between, they may find similar work or not work at all. During production they may be busier than they would like, but they know it won't last forever, so they handle it.

Free Days, Focus Days, and Buffer Days.®

The one thing to remember when exploring your post-retirement employment options is to keep flexible, be willing to adjust your skill set, and not fear the future.

Time management can be one challenge when going from an externally structured day to suddenly being in control of all your own time. A tool that has completely altered my relationship to time is The Entrepreneurial Time System,® a concept created by Dan Sullivan, as part of his Strategic Coach® program. This system was designed to increase an entrepreneur's personal freedom while still generating the most results for her business, but the concept can benefit anyone.

The Entrepreneurial Time System® divides your time into three specific types of days—Free Days, Focus Days, and Buffer Days.® Splitting your time into three distinct "black and white" days, rather than having all of your days blur into "gray," frees up energy and allows you to concentrate on what is most important to you and your goals.

As a retiree, you may treat every day the same: doing a few chores, having a fun outing, killing some time reading, and then getting up the next day and doing it all over again. This might work well for a few months, but after a while it can become boring.

Instead, consider putting all your "chore" work into one day. This is what Dan Sullivan refers to as a *Focus Day.*® You are expected to get results—so get up, go to "work," and get it done.

Then, set aside one full day for fun. This will be your *Free Day.* Literally, from the time you wake up until the time you go to bed, only do things that you totally love and get you energized.

Then, plan a *Buffer Day* before each of your Focus or Free Days, to do all the things to prepare for a great Focus Day—like go to the store, get your bank statements together, or organize your tools—and all the things to prepare for a great Free Day—like find the map for a hike, prepare food, or pull out your backpack.

What qualifies for a Free or Focus day will differ for each person. Mowing the lawn may be considered fun for one person, while for another it's a chore. Only you can say what needs to be done on your Free, Focus, and Buffer Days.® Also, if there is a "significant other" in your house, plan to spend some days together, some apart, but most importantly, all of them as coordinated as possible.

Change Is Inevitable. Struggle Is an Option.

The transition from full-time to part-time, freelance, or volunteer work can be challenging and scary. The cultural landscape of 45 years earlier, when our working lives began, has usually changed dramatically—for better or worse—by the time we retire. But take heart that, as the saying goes, change is inevitable; struggle is an option. Change can be disconcerting, but it needn't be overwhelming or bad.

Economically, at least, there is reason to be optimistic: At a recent Association of Financial Planners meeting, Dennis Stearns, head of Stearns Financial Services Group, identified eight burgeoning economic trends he believes have the potential of adding $1 trillion to the global economy. Among them, he asserts:[7]

- A huge market exists for vocational retraining and skill development as U.S. workers continue to suffer from structural unemployment and being untrained for emerging technology jobs in high demand.

- Thirty percent or more of traditional careers will be outsourced, marginalized, or cease to exist completely .

- Those 30 percent will be replaced by new employment stemming from the new tech economy .

- Those willing to adapt and retool their skill sets will ride this change to new and rewarding careers.

In his *Inside Information* article covering Stearns's presentation, Bob Veres writes, "… inevitably, if you try to extrapolate the future from the obvious situation today, you'll get it wrong. Change can be discontinuous and dramatic, and the controlling events are usually coming out of left field."[8]

Change can be scary, but we can make that change positive and exhilarating instead of distressing. Change can be daunting, but it is necessary in this human life, at retirement and beyond. To remain relevant, to truly keep and feel alive, transformation and change are essential.

"When you're through changing,
you're through."
~ *Bruce Barton*

"I work part time and don't make a lot of money, but I save a ton because I don't have time to shop anymore!"
~ *Sue Hartnett, who retired and then went back to work*

Retirement Profile: Andrew A. McVeigh (1921–2011)
Plant Manager
"A Discovery of Regret"

Andrew A. McVeigh retired at the age of 65, after having been employed by Armour Foods for 35 years and Swift Foods for seven. At the time of his retirement, he had been a plant manager of a pork slaughterhouse in South Dakota for 11 years. McVeigh took an aged plant that had been budgeted to lose money and turned it into one of the most successful plants in the company. His children always thought their father enjoyed his retirement—two and a half decades of it by the time he passed away. But in a conversation with him towards the end of his life, they were surprised to learn otherwise. McVeigh told them that retiring early was one of the worst decisions he had ever made, and he regretted it. If he could have done it over, he would have continued to work for five to ten more years. During his first years of retirement, he said, he was depressed and bored, not sure what to do with his time. Eventually, McVeigh became very involved at church, with a local food bank, and some other activities that worked his way out of his funk.

The lesson from Andrew McVeigh is to reconsider a vision of retirement. Think long and hard about what it will mean for you, given your personality. If you are highly active and involved in your work, don't suddenly bring it to a complete halt. You can't do something for most of your life, have it abruptly end, and expect no loss of purpose. If your career or work must come to an end as you know it, plan on replacing it with lesser work or volunteer activities—leisure alone doesn't typically provide long-term satisfaction. Even if you have not been highly active in your career or have been dreaming of days void of any obligations, a sudden lack of purpose or direction may be more challenging than you think.

—As told by Mr. McVeigh's son Andy

Retirement Profile: Viktor Frankl (1905–1997) Psychoanalyst, Influential Author, and Holocaust Survivor "Choose Your Attitude!"

Life today is tough, no question. So many of us deal with financial stress, families that are broken or scattered, careers that may not be our first choice, governments that may be inefficient or corrupt.... So, when we feel despondent and angry, even bitter and hopeless, it's justified, right?

Wrong!

Take Viktor Frankl—if ever there was a man who had the right to carry bitterness and resentment through life, it was he. With a brilliant and inquiring mind, and a shining career as a leading psychiatrist, Frankl's world came crashing down as the Nazis took over his native Austria. For three years he endured the Auschwitz concentration camps, where his pregnant wife, mother, father, and brother died in the gas chambers.

Frankl survived and, amazingly, went on to live without bitterness and rancor. After being liberated from the camps, Frankl chose to remain in Austria but *not* a prisoner of his horrific past. Frankl wrote his most famous book, *Man's Search for Meaning*, in a period of less than two weeks. In it he wrote, "Everything can be taken from a man, but one thing: the last of the human freedoms—to choose one's attitude in any given set of circumstances, to choose one's own way."

Frankl provided therapy to fellow prisoners in the camps. Referring to two suicidal inmates who felt they had nothing left to live for, he later wrote, "In both cases, it was a question of getting them to realize that life was still expecting something from them; something in the future was expected of them."

And, looking forward, he noted, "We can discover meaning in life in three different ways: (1) by creating a work or doing a deed; (2) by experiencing something or encountering someone; and (3) by the attitude we take toward unavoidable suffering."

According to a September 4, 1997 *New York Times* article, even before his transformative experiences in the concentration camps, Frankl had "evolved the theory... that the search for value and meaning in the circumstance of one's life was the key to psychological well-being."

Frankl died in 1997 at the age of 92, still actively teaching, debating, thinking and contributing to society.

> > > > > > > > > CHAPTER 5

SAVE 20 PERCENT
OF YOUR INCOME

"The question isn't at what age I want to retire, it's at what income."

—*George Foreman*

In the preceding chapters, we've explored a lot about instinctive purpose, finding your calling, realizing your passions, and focusing on your strengths. All fabulous pursuits, but these worthy endeavors need time, space, and trial and error to blossom into being.

And time, space, and trial and error are things you don't have if your attention is still absorbed in paying rent, anticipating the utility bill, and trading time for money.

Having money set aside to pursue your passions, navigate change, and weather *all* the storms in life can be the difference between a drudge-filled achy slog at retirement and an ease-filled, comfortable transition to an inspired, exhilarating, and purpose-driven second act.

That is why I'm devoting this and the next chapter to the nitty-gritty, nuts and bolts, hardcore, brass tacks of saving—specifically, saving for retirement.

Saving sometimes feels like a quaint, antiquated notion in our society. With huge financial institutions fiercely and relentlessly promoting the advantages of living with debt, living beyond our means has almost become the default in our culture.

But living beyond our means can cause a distress and discomfort that far outweigh the benefits of whatever fleeting satisfaction the product of that debt can bring.

In my Prosperity Economics book *Busting the Financial Planning Lies*, I put it this way:

Saving—Asserting Self-Discipline

If work is the necessary action to rise from Poverty, what action is needed to go beyond Subsistence living?

In response to this question, potential clients—that is, those looking for "financial planning"—often offer the following statements:

- I need a better job.
- I need a better education, so I can earn more money.
- I need to invest.

These answers miss the mark. In virtually every circumstance, the crucial action in rising above Subsistence to Comfort is not a matter of making more money or getting a better rate of return. It's about learning to live on less than you earn and keeping the excess. That's a long phrase for "saving." Just like consistent work provides a 99 percent assurance of the avoidance of Poverty, consistent practice of financial self-discipline is a sure-fire strategy for long-term financial Comfort.

Saving Is the Financial "Quantum Leap"

It might be simple, but deciding to consistently save is the financial "quantum leap" most people never take. Willingness to work requires only the acceptance of external discipline. Saving, on the other hand, demands self-discipline.

However, most of us are not naturally inclined to exercise self-control. As we earn more, we usually spend more. This is a human tendency—our spending expands in proportion to the money available—that some people never resist and never change. No matter how much they earn, they continue living at a Subsistence level. Saving, then, is not so much a matter of available income as it is an issue of self-control.

Compared to the benefits of working, the payoff for saving takes a little longer. With work, most of us see the rewards on a weekly, biweekly, or monthly basis when we get paid. With saving, it's conceivable the benefits may not be fully realized until the end of your working lifetime.

Initially, savings often don't move us ahead as much as they keep us from sliding back to Poverty when unexpected expenses occur. It is frustrating to see a year's worth of savings used up for a home repair, an automobile down payment, or a family emergency. Even though we mentally acknowledge our savings made the situation better because we didn't have to borrow, it's discouraging to see our progress toward Comfort and Prosperity deferred.

In order for saving to really become a progressive action (moving you up the Financial Ladder) instead of a defensive one (keeping you from Poverty), a substantial amount of earnings must be designated as savings. From our experience, those who discipline themselves to save 10–20 percent of their earnings will almost always achieve a level of financial Comfort. It's not a scientifically derived number, but I put forward this 10–20 percent range for two reasons.

First, earning and spending seem to be proportional. As mentioned above, when you make more, you spend more. But those earning a middle-class income don't usually have upper-class spending habits. (If they do, Poverty is on the horizon.) So wherever you are on the earning scale, 10–20 percent saving should be enough to provide not only a cushion that keeps you from sliding backward, but also create a growing reserve that moves you forward. (As far back as Genesis in the Old Testament, Joseph tells the Egyptians that they should set aside a fifth of their harvest—20 percent—to provide enough security against a coming famine.)

Second, the savings number will fluctuate depending on how quickly you want to progress toward Comfort and what standard of living you define as being comfortable. "Early Comfort" means faster accumulation. Additionally, a Comfort level that just means not having to work may not be as expensive as a Comfort level that allows for a lot of play.

But whether you think the saving percentage should be 10 percent or 20, current U.S. savings rates say volumes about why so few Americans will ever reach Comfort, even at retirement. As a whole, a large percentage of the population just isn't willing to exercise the self-discipline and delay gratification.

So, self-discipline and delaying gratification, even just a little bit, can banish the discomfort of debt, ease the transitions of life at every stage, and shore up the walls of your foundation so that, when the inevitable storms of life hit, poverty is not just around the corner.

"All right," he continued, "now I shall tell thee the first remedy I learned to cure a lean purse. Do exactly as I have suggested…. For every ten coins thou placest within thy purse take out for use but nine. Thy purse will start to fatten at once and its increasing weight will feel good in thy hand and bring satisfaction to thy soul."

~ *George S. Clason in* The Richest Man in Babylon

Although our *Busting the Financial Planning Lies* excerpt and *The Richest Man in Babylon* quote both suggest a savings rate as low as 10 percent, I urge you to save 20 percent.

I recommend this not only to boost your retirement savings but, as I've said, to help with life's expenses all along the way. Once you begin paying for car repairs, appliance replacements, medical bills, holiday gifts, and even the occasional vacation with cash, you'll begin to realize how good the "increasing weight of your fattening purse" actually feels.

So, with that, let's launch into the aforementioned Truth Concepts calculations I promised, where we'll uncover the *whole* truth about your money. The lies of both financial planning and retirement are many and varied, and I intend to bust them with some hard, cold, detailed number crunching.

The Whole Truth

The quandary of planning to be poor

Financial plans often assume that retirees will be willing and able to reduce their lifestyle expenses to 80 percent of their previous working income. While this may be logical in some way—children may be grown and mortgages paid off—in others it's hard to fathom. High-ticket items like medical expenses and long-term care kick in at retirement age. Moreover, starting a new business, learning a new skill, travel, and sometimes even volunteer work may require financial resources. So I am not a proponent of the "reduce your lifestyle expenses to 80 percent" rule. However, because this number has become so standard in the financial planning industry, I'll use it to illustrate our examples.

Inflation

It is an overlooked fact among most people that inflation is the enemy of true wealth creation. And thus, many people fail to truly account for it when planning their retirement savings. For those of you who have reached a certain age, you'll remember a time when candy bars were 25 cents. Today, you can find that same brand of candy bar in vending machines for $1.00 or more—same candy bar, same vending machines, just 300 percent more expensive today than previously. *That's* inflation.

The official number reported for annual inflation is currently 3.2 percent. It is likely that you, individually, have no influence over the course of this phenomenon, so there's no use fighting it or minimizing it in an attempt to make investment returns look better. What you must do, however, is account for it—in your saving, in your budgeting, and in your retirement planning.

The tracking of inflation is quite astounding. The U.S. Department of Labor's Bureau of Labor Statistics (BLS) has been recording the prices of approximately 80,000 goods and services in the American economy for more than a century, since 1913. A table containing the history of these indexed prices, and their percent change, can be found both within the Truth Concepts software and at the Bureau of Labor Statistics website.[9]

Now, let's run some simple calculations to illustrate the impact of inflation over time.

Crunching the numbers

Let's say you work for one of those companies that still provides a defined pension benefit, and you are close to age 55. You're thinking of retiring because you've been told your pension will be $3,000 a month, and you know you can live on that—today.

Life expectancy is increasing, and the likelihood that you will live into your 80s or even 90s is evermore probable, so let's see what that $3,000 a month will buy you in 30 years:

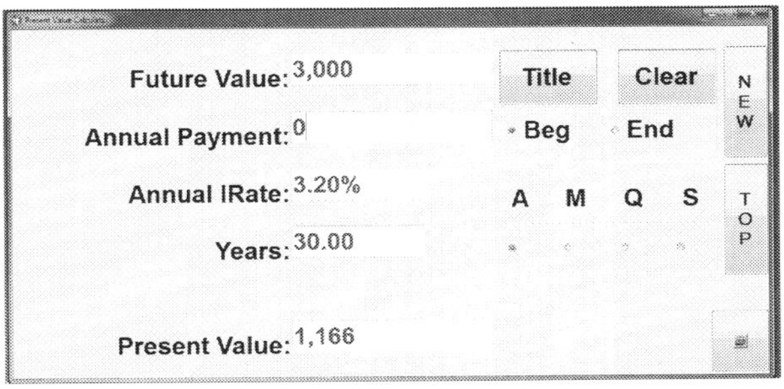

Figure 1

Figure 1 shows us that by age 85, your $3,000 per month will only buy what $1,166 buys today—an over 60 percent loss in your pension's value over 30 years.

While this is painful to consider, credible cases have been made that the official inflation rate is actually understated, and because 3.2 percent is only an average, the goods and services you *individually* buy may make your personal inflation rate higher. So let's look at a modest increase to a 4 percent inflation rate (Figure 2).

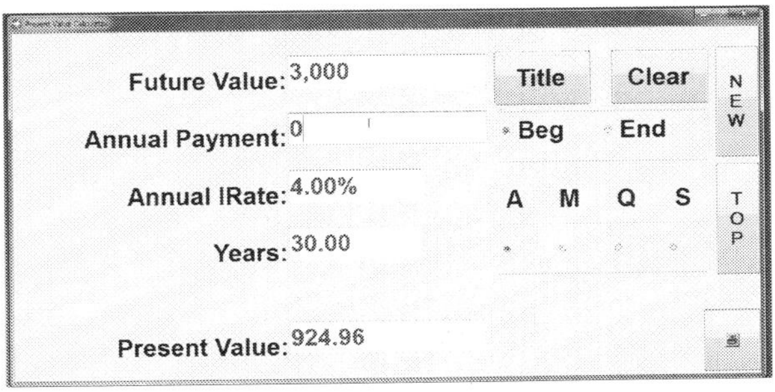

Figure 2

OUCH!

Even though the check will still read $3,000, it will only spend like $924.96 does today—an almost 70 percent loss in buying power over 30 years. This is not an easy dilemma to solve. The only way to address it is to have more money set aside or earn more income. Inflation is like a stealth tax because we don't really see it on a statement anywhere and it sneaks up on you over time.

The preceding examples looked at guaranteed pension income, something increasingly less common in America today. What if, however, like so many of us, your retirement savings is up to you alone? What if your retirement savings is pretty much all you'll have at retirement? Then, it's all the more important to factor inflation in accurately.

In Figure 3, let's presume the following factors. Our investor:

- earns $50,000 a year,
- has no existing assets,
- only saves 10 percent a year,
- is currently age 30,
- will work to age 60, and
- will experience a 3.2 percent average inflation rate.

According to Figure 3, our investor would need an annual income of $102,908 by age 60 to maintain the same buying power as $40,000 ($50,000 x 80 percent = $40,000) does today. And the $102,908 would need to increase an average of a 3.2 percent each year just to keep up with inflation after retirement.

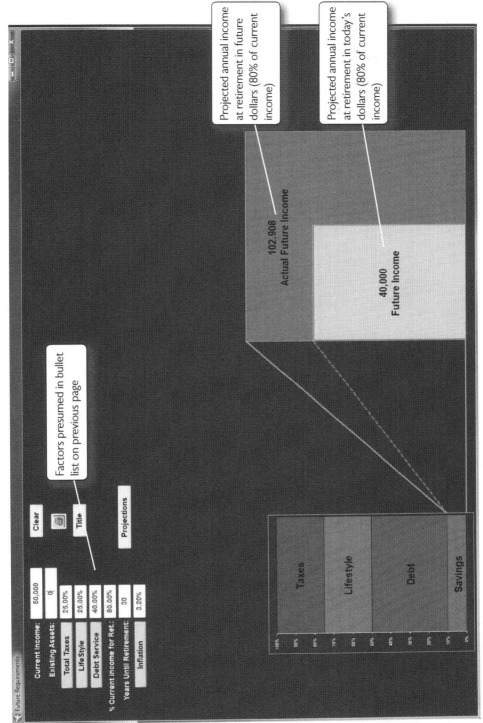

Figure 3

The previous calculation showed us how much income our investor needed to keep up with inflation after 30 years, but it didn't tell us how he is going to get there. To do this, let's look at some other factors. Figure 4 demonstrates that our investor would need to reach a $3,430,281 account balance, worth only $1,333,333 today, to generate his 80 percent income target of $102,908 per year (a 3 percent annual withdrawal).

For this to work, however, the account would need to earn *15.52 percent every single year, without any fluctuation, from age 30 to 60.* Then, in order to maintain that same lifestyle, with income rising annually to meet inflation, from age 60 to 90, the account would have to earn 6.39 percent annually, growing to $8,825,119. Of course, these are ridiculous rates of return that not even Bernie Madoff would have promised. But tragically, by not saving enough, investors try to make up for a lack of savings with aggressive and unrealistic growth strategies that backfire in the long run, leaving them with even less.

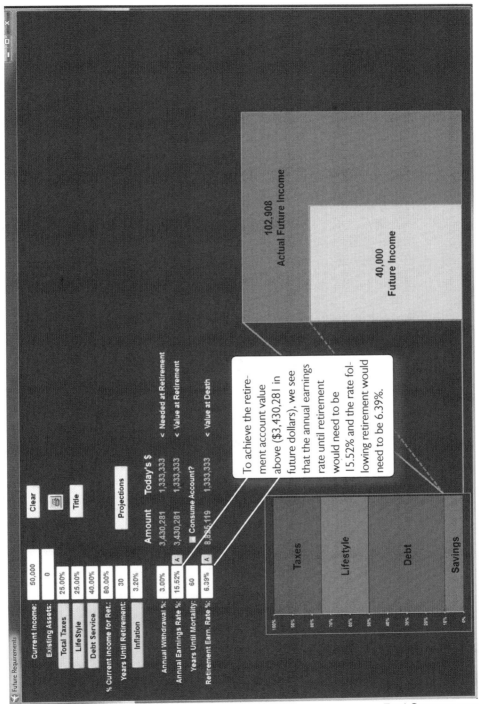

Figure 4

Figure 4 assumed our investor, at age 90, left $8,825,119 to his heirs. If he decided not to leave anything to inheritance, and instead consume the entire account, Figure 5 shows us that his retirement earnings rate could decrease to 2.47 percent.

Faulty assumptions

Financial planning makes assumptions about your future in ways that may be mathematically correct but are not realistic, like a 15.52 percent annual earnings rate. The graphs and charts may be pretty, but they don't reflect life. Although I used specific input variables in the preceding examples, I still contend it is very dangerous to assume interest rates, tax rates, inflation rates, and time frames, as they can be misleading and provide a false peace of mind. Our society today is changing so fast that it is ridiculous to assume anything will stay the same for more than a few years.

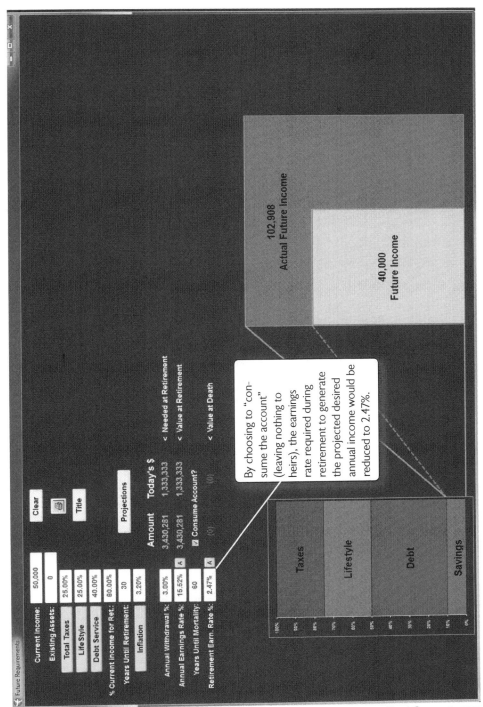

TruthConcepts.com

Figure 5

Misleading averages

Another of the financial-planning industry's tricky tactics is the use of averages to promote returns instead of revealing the actual returns their products earn. An example of this, exaggerated for clarity, is illustrated in the following scenario and Figure 6.

Pretend someone offers you a mutual fund with an average return of 25 percent. Sounds pretty good. So, you put $100,000 in the fund and watch for two years to get your results.

You can see in Figure 6 that the average yield is in fact 25 percent, but your *actual* yield is 0 percent because you still only have your $100,000 in the account. This is because your fund earned 100 percent the first year and *negative 50 percent* the second. Quick math shows that 100 percent plus negative 50 percent, divided by 2, equals 25 percent.

To put it another way, $100,000 earning 100 percent for year one grows to $200,000, but then gets cut in half when the fund loses 50 percent in year two. So at the end of year two, you are back to the $100,000 you started with, even though the "average yield" really was 25 percent. This is how the mutual fund industry calculates their returns!

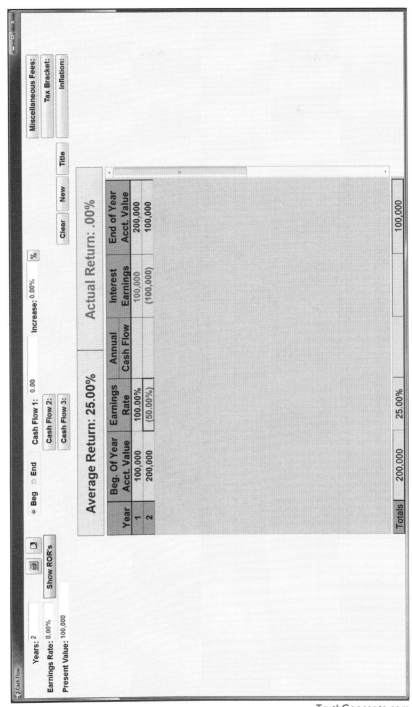

Figure 6

Okay, you might say, at least you haven't lost any money. But, as we've seen previously, only looking at the earnings rate of an investment leaves out key components that dramatically impact your balance, whether you choose to account for them or not. So, as we have in previous examples, let's factor in management fees, taxes, and inflation in Figure 7.

At the top right of Figure 7, we've set management fees at 2 percent, taxes at 25 percent (a blended rate of income and capital gains, for this example), and inflation at 3.2 percent. You'll see that after only two years of investment, your account is now only worth $79,134 —*an actual loss of 11.04 percent*. Hardly the 25 percent average you'd hoped for or expected.

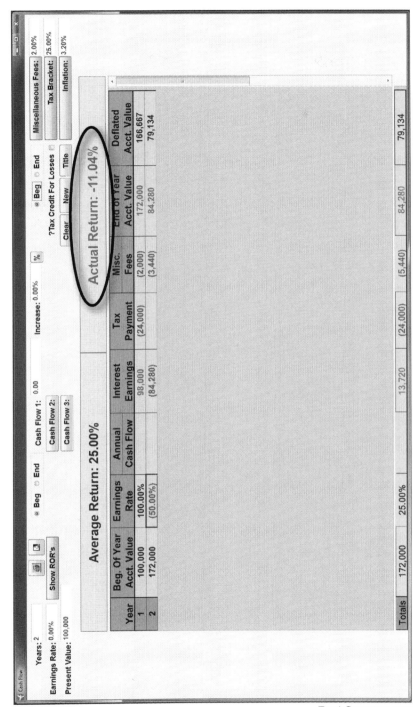

Figure 7

Guessing about your age of retirement and passing

Financial planning assumes you know when you will want to stop working and when you will die. Both are really total guesses, and yet they are used to make major decisions around life and money. The government dictates we *can't touch* our retirement dollars until age 59½ and then we *have to* start using them at 70½. But what do these ages have to do with our lives in any way? They are simply arbitrary and arguably outdated.

Statistics are showing more and more people in the United States living past age 100. Yet, most financial plans still assume death at 85 or 90. We can look at a male age 60 on the life expectancy chart in Figure 8 and know that this means he has only a *50 percent chance* of dying by age 82, the life expectancy year listed on the chart. And the longer you live, the longer you are likely to live—the 60-year-old man in Figure 8 has a 50 percent chance of living to age 82, but the 75-year-old man has a 50 percent chance of living to nearly age 88.

By the way, Figure 8 is the most recent Mortality Table used by the life insurance industry—and it's from 2001! That industry doesn't update their tables very often, so it's easy to see how this information could already be outdated as of the writing of this book. But regardless, the bottom line is that you'll probably live longer than you think. In order to have a higher quality of life for a longer time, you'll want to factor that in to your retirement planning.

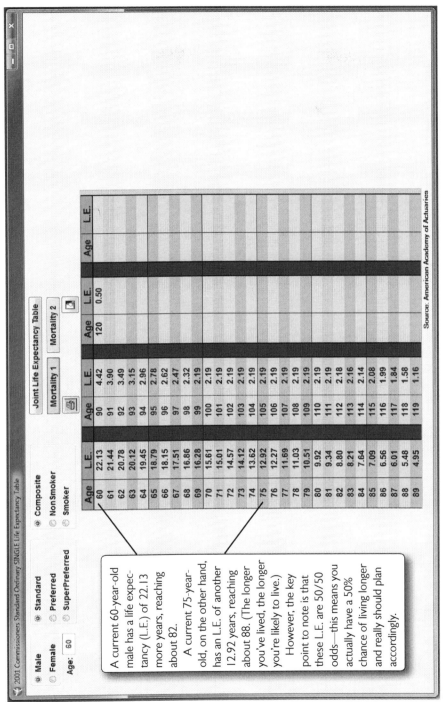

Figure 8

TruthConcepts.com

Not realistically accounting for inflation

Another characteristic of inflation is that the longer money sits, the more impact inflation has on it. Figure 9 represents an existing $100,000 account balance where $20,000 is being added to the account every year and a 3.2 percent inflation rate applied.

At the bottom of Figure 9, at year 25, you can see that while your account statement would read $600,000, after 25 years of 3.2 percent inflation, it would only spend like $272,998.

"Give yourself all the time you can
and never forget the risk of inflation."
~ *John C. Bogle*
Founder, The Vanguard Group+

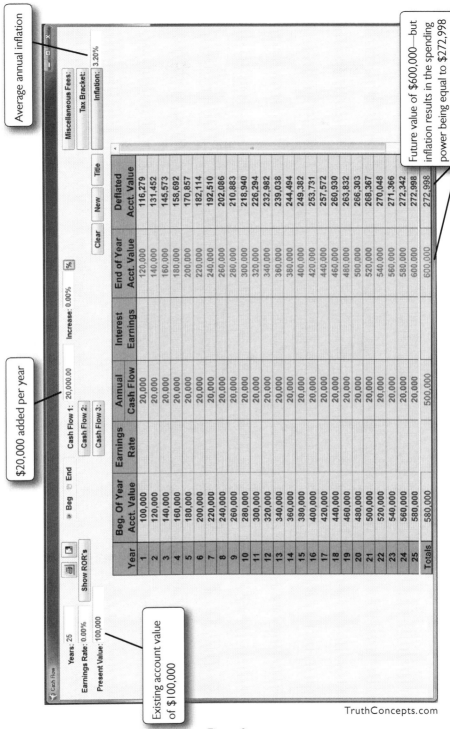

Average annual inflation

$20,000 added per year

Existing account value of $100,000

Future value of $600,000—but inflation results in the spending power being equal to $272,998 in today's money.

TruthConcepts.com

Figure 9

Trying to beat inflation with savings

One other financial planning lie I'd like to bust is that if you increase your savings rate by the rate of inflation every year, you'll conquer the inflation problem. However, Figure 9 also shows us that inflation works on the *whole account value, not just your contributions,* so simply increasing your savings rate does not solve the problem.

To illustrate this, in Figure 10, I've increased the $20,000 annual contributions by 3.2 percent each year. Nevertheless, it still doesn't make the account value feel like present-day $848,638. Instead, it feels like $386,127.

The only things that solve the problem are more money at work or more *you* at work for a longer time.

Inflation is a tricky thing, and many financial calculators do not factor it in. Bear in mind that there are only a few things that benefit from inflation: fixed mortgage payments, fixed life insurance premiums, and people who keep on working.

The preceding charts used the Bureau of Labor Statistic's official average inflation rate. The fact that prices are increasing incrementally may only seem like a vague, uneasy sensation to you, but when you look at all the effort that goes into calculating and quantifying the cost of living, you will know that inflation is a real, measureable, and definitive force on your money and your life, and must be accounted for.

In the next chapter, I'm going to address some guiding principles and practices that will not only help you account for inflation but put you on the road to make the most of your money throughout your life.

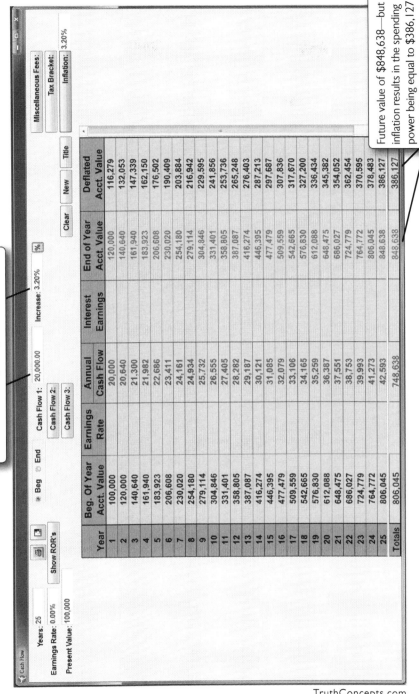

Same $20,000 added per year, but with an extra 3.2% annually to try to offset inflation

Future value of $848,638—but inflation results in the spending power being equal to $386,127 in today's money.

TruthConcepts.com

Figure 10

Retirement Profile: R. Nelson Nash (1931–)
Financial Crusader and Best-Selling Author
"Life Is Too Much Fun to Miss Out!"

Octogenarian R. Nelson Nash is a man who doesn't believe in retirement. "There is no way to convince me to retire! This life is too much fun to miss out!" he exclaimed in a December 2011 interview with the *Lara-Murphy Report* entitled "Austrian Economics + Whole Life = Infinite Banking Concept."

The originator of the Infinite Banking Concept, which promotes the use of whole life insurance to finance major expenses, Mr. Nash is a sought-after speaker, writer, and financial consultant.

In his view, the very idea of retirement is an anomaly. Nash exhorts that mankind needs a purpose in life and that government-legislated retirement ages are arbitrary. Germany's Chancellor Bismarck set the retirement age at 70, when the average life expectancy was far below. Similarly, Nash exclaims that when Social Security was introduced in the United States in 1937, placing the retirement age at 65, the average life expectancy was only 61 years.

Today, Americans' life expectancy is 79 to 80 years. On account of this, Nash believes there is no way Social Security can ever really work and give retirees an adequate living income.

Nash started his career as a forester for private companies in the early 1950s after graduating with a Bachelor of Science degree in Forestry from the University of Georgia. He subsequently served as a life insurance agent with Equitable of New York for 23 years and The Guardian Life for 12 years. His concept of Infinite Banking is described in his classic book, *Becoming Your Own Banker*, and is the basis for the roughly 50 seminars he delivers every year around the United States. To learn more about Nash's excellent strategy, one that aligns perfectly with Prosperity Economics, visit his website InfiniteBanking.org.

CHAPTER 6

THE REALITY OF
RETIREMENT PLANS

"Age is only a number, a cipher for the records. A man can't retire his experience. He must use it."

—Bernard Baruch, financier, investor,
philanthropist, and statesman

The Seven Principles of Prosperity

In *The Richest Man in Babylon*, George S. Clason relays in ancient parable: "I tell you, my students, a man's wealth is not in the coins he carries in his purse; it is the income he buildeth, the golden stream that continually floweth…."

Clason's work addresses many prosperity principles that go back to biblical times. In similar fashion, the Prosperity Economics Movement is based on Seven Principles of Prosperity that guide its direction and influence the investment advice it provides.

The Seven Principles of Prosperity are:

1. **Think**—Owning a prosperity mindset eliminates poverty; scarcity thinking keeps you stuck.
2. **See**—Increase your prosperity by adopting a macro-economic point of view: a perspective in which you can see how one economic decision affects all the others. Avoid micro-economic "tunnel-vision."
3. **Measure**—Awareness and measurement of opportunity costs enables you to mitigate, and sometimes recover them. Ignore this at your peril.

4. **Flow**—The true measure of prosperity is cash flow. Don't focus on net worth alone.

5. **Control**—Those with the gold make the rules; stay in control of your money rather than relinquishing control to others.

6. **Move**—The velocity of money is the movement of dollars through assets. Your money can move through your assets or toward them. Movement through assets accelerates prosperity; moving toward your assets—accumulation—slows it down.

7. **Multiply**—Prosperity comes readily when your money "multiplies," specifically when one dollar does many jobs. Your money is disabled when each dollar performs only one or two jobs.

Qualified Retirement Plans

With these principles in mind, I'll first address the ubiquitous, prolific, ever-present, American retirement savings vehicle: the 401(k) plan.

In 1978, Section 401(k) was added to the Internal Revenue Code, and currently, about half of all businesses in the United States offer 401(k) plans to workers.

It is the most well known of a number of "qualified" plans, which typically refer to investment accounts in which the principle and interest that accumulate over the years is tax deferred.

With a tax-deferred plan, instead of paying taxes every year on the money deposited and the interest accumulating in the account, you defer those taxes—postponing or delaying payment until you withdraw that money, sometimes decades later, at retirement. This allows what you would have paid in taxes to accrue interest right alongside your own net contributions.

Bear in mind, though, that you are not exempted or excused from paying taxes. You still have to pay them, either in one lump sum or in chunks, as you withdraw your money at, or over the course of, your retirement.

I've often seen clients mix up the terms tax deferment and tax deduction. The concepts are quite different, so let's discuss a bit of that difference now. A tax *deduction* is an expense subtracted from your annual income that ultimately reduces your tax liability—such as your mortgage interest, home office expenses, and unreimbursed auto usage for work purposes. Tax *deferment* is only a postponement or delay of taxes due. The advantage to this, as I mentioned earlier, is that those taxes can earn extra interest right alongside other 401(k) money, increasing the account's overall balance over time.

Unfortunately, although extra interest on tax-deferred principle is nice, it's important to remember that payments postponed to an unknown time in the future will be taxed at an unknown future tax rate—something that could be very advantageous or very detrimental. It's essentially a "loan" from the IRS—but at a to-be-determined rate! Obviously, that's not a financial arrangement a savvy person should take lightly or make without serious consideration.

Despite this, over the past thirty years, the perceived benefit of the 401(k) plan has become so engrained in American society that it is often considered a minimum requirement for recruiting and retaining employees. "Maxing out your 401(k)" is also the default advice from popular finance gurus, and qualified plans are the first thing that most people think of when they decide to save for the future. But are they really all they're cracked up to be?

The Seven Principles of Prosperity Test

Despite the pervasiveness and popularity of the 401(k) plan, it's important to challenge the assumption that a qualified plan is the best place to put your money while trying to build wealth. So, let's do this using the Prosperity Economics' Seven Principles of Prosperity test:

1. **Think**

   Does the 401(k) eliminate or reduce poverty thinking and lifestyle?

   A: Yes

   B: No

   Well, the answer is no… living an austere existence to save for the future on the premise that the joys of retirement will outweigh all the lost opportunities for reward, investment, and growth today is a poverty mindset.

2. **See**

   Consider the macro-perspective ("40,000-foot view"). How does the 401(k) affect your personal economic situation?

   A: It improves it

   B: It does not improve it

   Well, it *sounds* like it might improve it. You put some money away for retirement, and when you are ready to leave the working world, it's there for you. But wait. Things start looking quite different when you consider that (a) your income will be fully taxable at an unknown, to-be-determined rate; (b) your social security benefits could be taxed; (c) it won't provide any disability protection if you are hurt and can no longer work; (d) you can't collateralize it; and (e) your information is made public in the ERISA Red Book.

3. **Measure**

    Are you aware of the 401(k)'s opportunity costs? Have you measured them?

    A: Yes

    B: No

    The answer is *maybe*. You might be aware of your opportunity costs, but if you really *are* measuring them, you'd see this one as a no-brainer. By putting the money from your earnings into the 401(k), you are giving up the capital-gain tax treatment offered by other investments. As the money is not liquid, it can't be redeployed for other use, and the management costs are significant.

4. **Flow**

    Does the opportunity result in cash stagnating or flowing?

    A: Flowing

    B: Stagnating

    This one is clear. The 401(k) plan promotes a *hoarding and stagnation mentality*. You are looking to benefit from the reinvestment of interest, so the opportunity for cash flow is eliminated. Locking up that capital is helpful *for your financial advisors* but detrimental to you, your financial security, power, and prosperity potential.

5. **Control**

    Will you remain in control of your capital with a 401(k) or lose control of it?

    A: Remain in Control

    B: Lose Control

    Simple: You'll lose control of it. Your capital cannot be leveraged as collateral for other investments unless you want to "borrow" a limited amount at a steep cost, possible penalty, and with very specific structured repayment terms. Moreover, not only does your dollar do only one job here, you lose most of the control over where it is invested and when it can distributed.

6. **Move**

    Does this opportunity enable the velocity of money through your assets or toward them to accumulate?

    A: It moves through

    B: It accumulates

    This test is pretty self-evident, too. Money accumulates here and is not moving at all. When it isn't moving, it cannot go through assets, only toward them.

7. **Multiply**

    Does your money do several "jobs" with this opportunity or only one?

    A: Several jobs

    B: Only one

    Only one or two jobs here, and the tax-deferral benefit is not really a job at all—it's just a way of delaying an inevitable expense.

So, as you can see, with qualified plans, you can easily move out of the prosperity paradigm and into one of poverty without even really knowing it.

Qualified Retirement Plans—the Whole Truth and Nothing but the Truth

Employers, retirement advisors, and the hard-working folks they advise often tout the incomparable merits of a 401(k) plan. Likewise, they praise IRAs, SEP IRAs, Simple IRAs, 403(b)s, profit-sharing, pension plans, and other investment vehicles that offer deferred taxes on contributions. So, for the rest of this chapter, let's take a look at the whole truth of this assertion, by following a series of calculations using a theoretical retirement plan.

Earnings

Truth concepts

Let's say we have a hardworking individual, Penelope, who is currently 35 and single. She has worked and saved diligently throughout the past twelve years and currently has a balance of $100,000 in her 401(k). In Figure 11, we're going to take that $100,000 and project out through age 64. We will assume an earnings rate of 8 percent, year after year. Bear in mind that this is an actual earnings rate, not the average rate so often advertised in a retirement fund prospectus. (Review the section on "Misleading averages" in Chapter 5 for more about *actual* versus *average*.)

The earnings rate is displayed in the top left of the chart, and is another term for interest rate; it is the interest Penelope earns each and every year on the various funds inside her 401(k).

Conversely, the rate of return, displayed in the white box toward the top right of the chart, is Penelope's overall profit earned on the entire account, including all costs, fees, taxes, and matches. While the earnings rate is specific to the funds inside her 401(k), the rate of return is Penelope's overall profit gained from the entire investment scenario.

Figure 11 illustrates what $100,000 earning 8 percent over 30 years would grow to.

After 30 years, with the $100,000 left untouched and no further contributions made after age 35, the gross account value, displayed in the white box at the bottom of the chart, grows to $1,006,266. Because there are no other variables considered, the earnings rate and overall rate of return are equal.

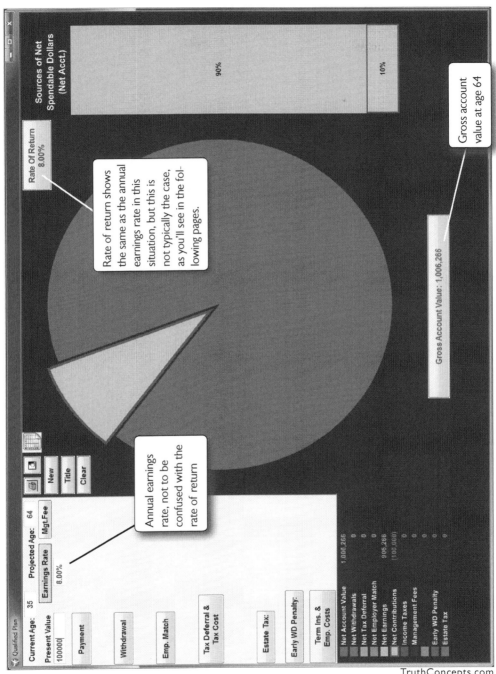

Figure 11

Now, in Figure 12, let's say Penelope continues to add to her $100,000 after age 35. In fact, let's say she adds another $833 each month, every month, totaling $10,000 per year. Because Penelope has developed the habit of saving, let's say she continues her contributions each month, without fail, through age 64.

Penelope's diligence in saving grows her gross account value to $2,229,724.

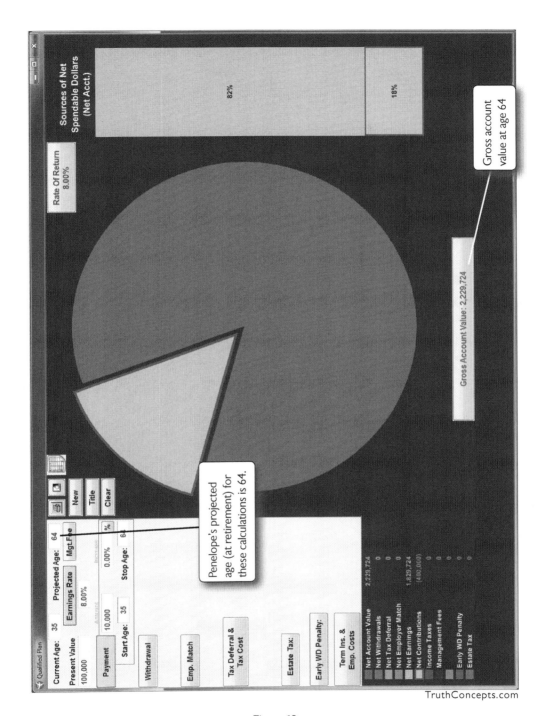

TruthConcepts.com

Figure 12

Employer match

Another reason people are so eager to put money into qualified retirement plans is the employer match commonly provided. We often hear people say they are getting a 50-percent match—and they seem pretty impressed by that. But you may want to look closely at your documents. An employer match is usually capped at a maximum amount, either a percentage of income or occasionally a flat dollar amount. In this case, let's assume Penelope's employer match maxed out at $2,500 per year. Remember, that match is only 50 percent in our scenario, so an extra $1,250 per year will go into her account from her employer—less than a month and a half of what Penelope herself contributes.

Figure 13 shows us that with the employer match beginning at age 35, Penelope's gross account value grows to $2,382,657. Because the employer match is not Penelope's own money, it does increase her rate of return, but only slightly, from 8.00 to 8.29 percent.

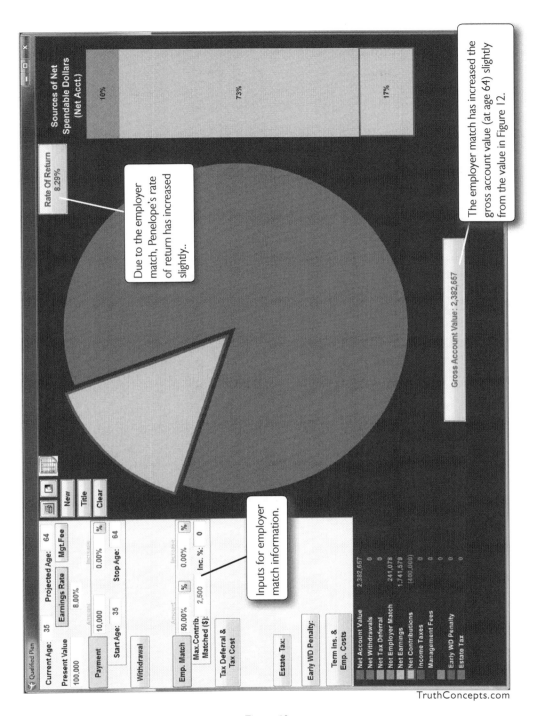

Figure 13

Tax deferral

As I discussed earlier, one of the primary reasons 401(k)s are so lauded is for their tax deferral component.

Penelope, after all her tax deductions, falls in the 25.00 percent tax bracket. Thus, instead of paying the $2,500 in taxes owed on her $10,000 per year contributions (not to be confused with the $2,500 employer match just discussed), those taxes are deferred or delayed until the time she withdraws her money—the $2,500 stays in her account each year, accruing interest right alongside her own net contributions. So, while her net contribution is only $7,500, she gets the benefit of the whole $10,000 accruing to the growth.

> It's important to note that the calculator only determines the Rate of Return based on Penelope's portion of the contribution into the plan—not the government-provided tax deferral.

Thus, at the bottom left of Figure 14, we see that the $2,500 of deferred taxes, factored separately, compounding at 8 percent interest for 30 years, has grown to $491,796.

So, when you add the tax-deferral amount plus the interest accrued on it for 30 years, Penelope's rate of return rises to 9.52 percent.

You may think, *Not all so bad. What's wrong with a 9.52-percent return? That's why I'm placing my money in a qualified plan in the first place.* Well, I'd like that to be the end of the story. But, as you know, the Prosperity Economics Movement is about telling the whole truth about your money, so let's continue to the next page.

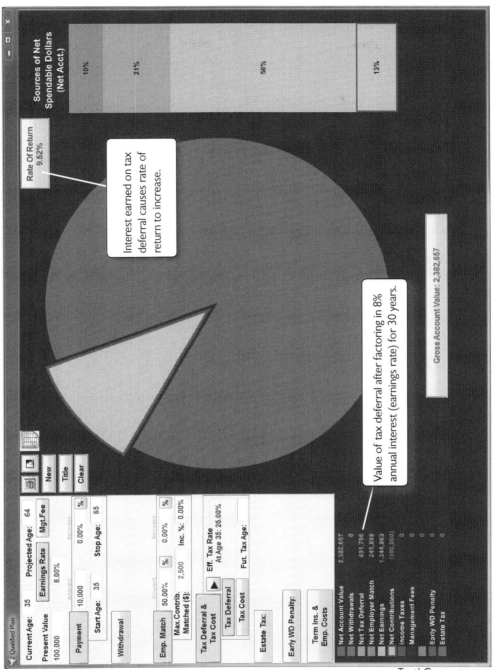

Figure 14

Costs

Unfortunately, the tax-deferral benefits and employer match are not the only components of qualified retirement plans. There are others—costs that come with all that automated, no-brainer investing. Let's examine how these impact the value of the plan.

Management fees

A conservative figure for qualified account management fees is 2.5 percent per year. Seems small, even nominal. (They're actually higher than typical fees charged outside of qualified plans, where market forces tend to keep fees lower than what the "more captive" qualified plan customer pays.) These fees cover the cost of both managing the money and administering the plan itself. Keep in mind that these fees operate on the entire account value and are taken out every three months over 30 years. Figure 15 shows us the impact:

After 30 years, with 2.5 percent of your gross account value taken out every year on a quarterly basis, you will have paid $439,204 in management fees. If we factor in the interest that $439,204 would have earned at 8 percent had it stayed in the account for 30 years, we arrive at a whopping $643,811—making the total cost of fees and their foregone interest an astonishing $1,083,015. This is the opportunity cost of investing in highly managed funds. And it's this opportunity cost that reduces Penelope's gross account value— originally $2,382,657—all the way down to $1,299,642.

Imagine losing nearly half of your total retirement savings, taken out in little bites every three months over 30 years. What could that money have done for you at the time? What could an extra $1,083,015 do for you later in life?

Because management fees are not your own money, they definitely affect your rate of return, which has now plunged from 9.48 percent in Figure 14 to 6.90 percent in Figure 15.

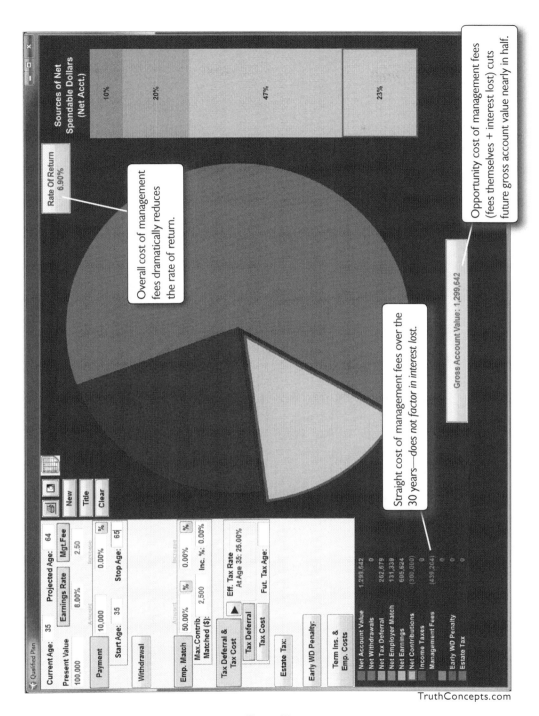

TruthConcepts.com

Figure 15

Tax cost upon withdrawal

But wait, there's more! Management fees are not the only costs to consider when evaluating your retirement saving options. Remember the snazzy tax-deferral advantage? Well, when it's time to withdraw, it's time to pay up. Upon withdrawal, qualified retirement savings are treated like ordinary income and taxed at whatever the income tax rate is at the time.

So, on the bottom left of Figure 16, we see that if Penelope withdraws her entire gross account value in one lump sum at age 65, she would have to pay $488,173 in income taxes, leaving her with a net account value of $811,469 for her retirement.

It's important to note that the age period from 35 to 64 for Penelope is 30 years, because it includes the beginning and ending years (i.e., age 35 *through* 64). So, for the purposes of illustration, Penelope would be withdrawing her full account on her 65th birthday.

Even though the account statement would still show a gross account value of $1,299,642, only $811,469 of that money is Penelope's to spend. Factoring in taxes brings the overall rate of return down to 4.80 percent.

As we saw earlier in Figure 14, the deferral of taxes owed on your contributions does result in a nice sum over the years. However, this might be a good time to talk about the philosophy behind qualified retirement accounts. While our retirement saver, Penelope, happily grew her annual $2,500 in deferred taxes to a decent result over 30 years, the government gained on this proposition as well. As you can see in Figure 16, Penelope's Net Tax Deferral is $159,404. Not bad. This is what she ultimately gained from the $2,500 per year in deferred taxes. However, by closing out this account at age 65, she'd pay $488,173 in income taxes—which means the government would get $415,673 more than it would have if Penelope had merely paid the $75,000 over time ($2,500 per year for 30 years).

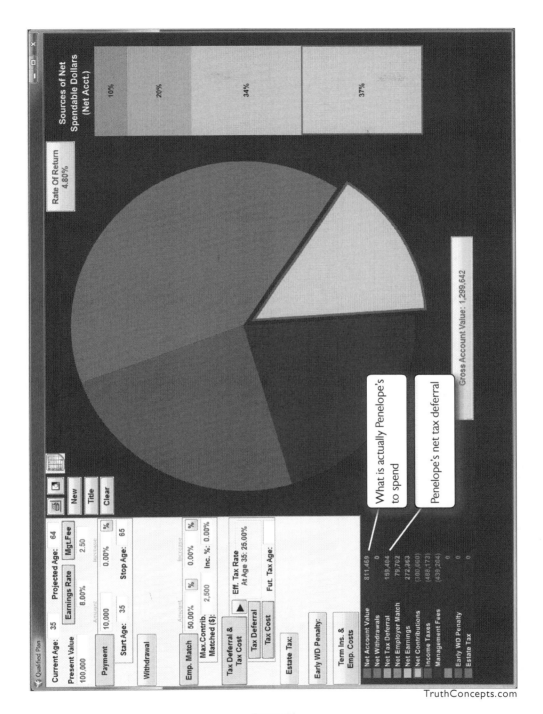

Figure 16

Withdrawing over time

When our clients see this huge tax liability, such as the $488,173 in Figure 16, they sometimes argue that they would never take their entire retirement savings out in one lump sum. Instead, they would take disbursements, with-drawing their savings in small chunks or install-ments every year over the course of their retire-ment. That's a very likely scenario, so let's see how taking yearly disburse-ments affects things.

Figure 17 shows a yearly disbursement of $98,823 beginning on Penelope's 65th birth-day. In this example, we assume that contribu-

> Many people are aware that taking distributions prior to reaching age 59½ will result in paying the tax rate at the time plus a 10 percent "early with-drawal" penalty. And some are aware that during the eleven-year period between 59½ and 70½, money may be withdrawn without penalty. Fewer, however, are aware that, by law, after age 70½, there is a 50 percent penalty for withdrawing less than the required minimum distributions. So, as of the date of this writing, if you don't want to incur a 50 percent penalty, you would have to start withdrawing money as of age 70½.

tions to the account stop at this point, but the remaining account value continues to grow and accrue interest over the next 20 years.

The $98,823 Penelope could withdraw every year (to zero out the account at age 85) is considered annual gross income, and her resulting net income would be taxed at whatever the correspond-ing tax rate is at the time. For simplicity, let's say she remains at the same $80,000 net income and 25 percent tax bracket we've used so far. The result is that her rate of return does get a bump up to 5.42 percent; however, this isn't a significant advantage over the 4.80 percent rate of return from the lump-sum scenario.

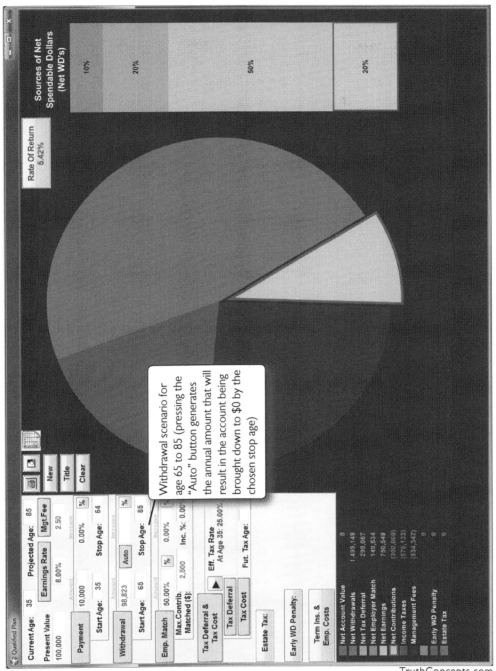

TruthConcepts.com

Figure 17

And what if our tax rate after retirement was lower, perhaps 21.21 percent, and we withdraw in installments? In Figure 18, we see that our rate of return creeps up just a tiny bit, from 5.42 to 5.71 percent—not a large improvement.

This may seem pretty good, and it's certainly better than your rate of return when withdrawing all at once—but keep reading, because we still haven't quite arrived at the whole truth yet.

Now is a good time to look again at the bar graph on the right. As I pointed out earlier, in Figures 11–14, this keeps track of our money (the sources of what we've actually earned in the account and what percentage they are of our net withdrawals from age 65 to 85). This breakdown shows that 18 percent of the money comes from our own net contributions, which corresponds to the $300,000 in the list in the bottom left of Figure 18. The largest block of 52 percent is the interest we earned ($844,415 at the bottom left). The 20 percent is both the tax deferral and the growth on the tax deferral by the end of the timeframe, $327,090. And finally, the 10 percent is the match and the growth on that employer match, $163,545.

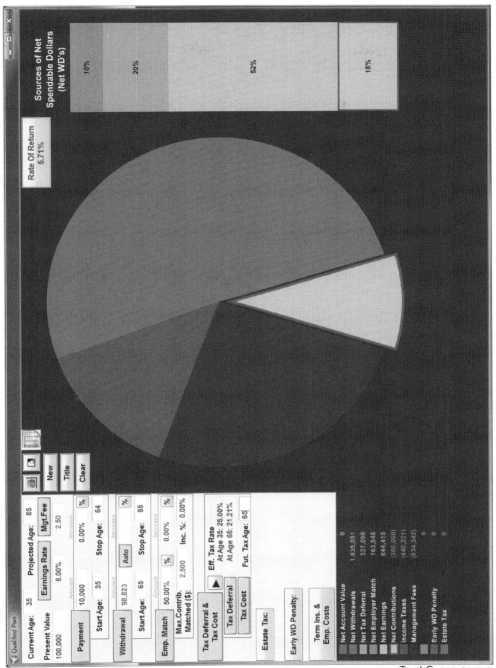

TruthConcepts.com

Figure 18

Six percent earnings rate

Thus far, I've used an exemplary earnings rate of 8 percent. In reality, expecting to earn this rate is too optimistic. Most accounts fluctuate, sometimes wildly, over time. So, what if your account only earns 6 percent year after year, with no down years, and you withdraw in installments to zero out the account by age 85? Figure 19 shows us the results.

Your overall rate of return drops to only 3.93 percent!

But I'm afraid that's not quite the end of it. There's one more variable we need to factor in when computing the end game of qualified retirement plans. It was heavily discussed in chapter 5, though I have yet to mention it here, and it is pivotal in grasping the whole truth about your money. It will wreak havoc on your retirement savings, and Penelope's, year after year. That factor is inflation. As I discussed in the preceding chapter, the official rate of inflation has averaged 3.23 percent the past century. Applied to our most recent rate of return (3.93 percent from Figure 19), Penelope's actual rate of return, adjusted for inflation, is little more than one half of one percent—0.70 percent, to be exact.

> "In time of universal deceit,
> telling the truth is a revolutionary act."
> ~ *George Orwell*

So, our dear Penelope—after 30 years of diligent saving, $1,083,015 in management fees, $488,173 in taxes, and an inflation rate of 3.23 percent—will earn less than a 1-percent rate of return on her retirement money.

And that is the whole truth about Penelope's money, and yours.

Not quite what the fund prospectus advertised, is it?

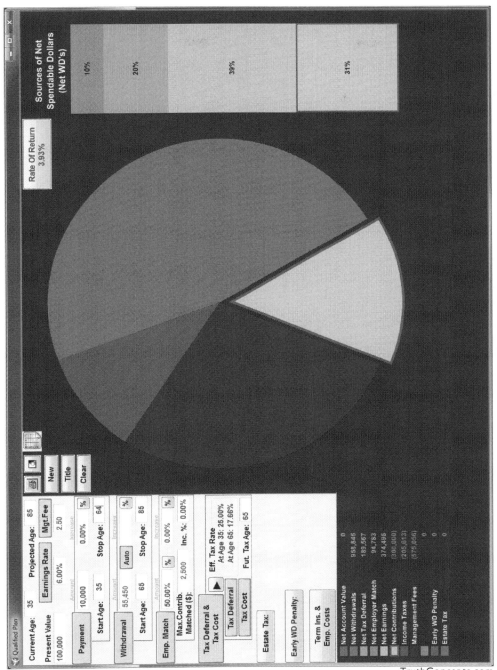

TruthConcepts.com

Figure 19

The 401(k) and other qualified plans have great marketing campaigns, but they are simply not the best place to put money while trying to build assets. And build assets you should. Certainly, a substantial employer match may make this situation more appealing, but even with a great match, the rules of qualified plans prevent your money from being used for much of your lifetime. This defies the founding principles of Prosperity Economics and may, in the worst case, back you and your family into a corner when the money is needed most.

Getting a CLUE

In addition to the Seven Principles of Prosperity, I also use the acrostic "CLUE":

- Control,
- Liquidity
- Use
- Equity

"Getting a CLUE" reminds us that we would like our savings and investment strategies to be: in our *Control*; *Liquid* and accessible; available for our *Use* before and after retirement; and *Equity* that's available to borrow against when need or opportunity strikes.

Qualified retirement plans like 401(k)s, with funds chosen by money managers, subjected to hefty fees and restrictions when using the money pre-retirement, and limited to only one job—saving for retirement—defy all these principles.

What Then? Where *Can* You Save?

Wealthy people have always practiced what we call Prosperity Economics. So to find the answer to the question, "Where can I save?" we have to look at how people built wealth prior to the existence and popularization of the 401(k). Prior to the financial planning industry, the most used strategies were "savings accounts, whole life insurance, and the home mortgage," according to Steve Utkus, director of the Vanguard Center for Retirement Research, as quoted in the book *Pound Foolish* by Helaine Olen.

While I do not recommend putting anything more than the first few thousand dollars of your emergency fund in a savings account, the three traditional assets named by Utkus—savings accounts, whole life insurance (the cash value portion), and homes (real estate)—demonstrate some profound similarities.

First, they are assets that allow people to build ownership. As I discussed in *Busting the Financial Planning Lies*, this is the step that allows you to go from Comfort to Prosperity on the Prosperity Ladder.

Second, these three assets fare much better than 401(k)s when measured against the CLUE principles:

Control: The owner of the accounts or homes controls the asset, as opposed to a money manager, a brokerage, a qualified plan administrator, the fickle market, or the ever-changing tax code.

Liquidity: A home can take months to sell, while bank accounts and whole life cash value are almost instantly liquid.

Use: The owner can use the asset, as opposed to an asset that remains in someone else's control.

Equity: Savings accounts, cash value in a whole life policy, and a home or other piece of real estate allow owners to build equity and to even collateralize or borrow against it.

Finally, high cash value insurance and real estate also prove to be solid assets under the Seven Principles of Prosperity test. For instance, the ability to grow and manage our own assets increases our ability to THINK from a Prosperous Mindset and SEE the big picture. Owning assets we can leverage allows us to MEASURE opportunity costs and keep more assets working for us. We can CONTROL and build cash FLOW with these assets, rather than having money locked away until we are 59½ or being forced to liquidate the assets before we are ready to do so. Whole life and real estate allow us to MOVE money *through* assets, not simply *to* assets. And finally, our dollars can MULTIPLY by doing many of jobs in both whole life insurance and in real estate.

Money Currents

William Keiper, in *Life Expectancy: It's Never To Late To Change Your Game*, put it this way: "The word 'currency' brings to mind currents: bodies of water or air moving in a specific direction, or in electricity, the flow of an electric charge through a particular medium. The word 'circulation' suggests what is really important in the pursuit of money: movement in the form of currency flowing through the entire financial system."

In no way do I suggest that saving and investing for retirement is a bad thing. It's not. It's very, very good. However, high-priced, inaccessible, and often opaque retirement funds are not the ideal way to go about this. It's a bad choice financially, and it's bad for you as well, emotionally, psychologically, physically, and spiritually.

Keiper continues, "Money has no real value if it stops circulating. It may provide the holder... with a psychological benefit of security or power... but it is stuck in the system and not creating optimal value.... Money in motion has more real value than money at rest. Money that is passing through is money that has a chance to multiply."

Find ways to keep your money moving through assets, such as savings accounts inside life insurance cash value, and "financial freedom" or "opportunity" accounts, set aside in investments that are liquid, transparent, and not tied up in the rules of qualified retirement plans.

In *The Ultimate Gift*, Jim Stovall writes, "Money is nothing more than a tool. It can be a force for good, a force for evil, or simply be idle." Don't let your money or your mind be idle. It takes some effort to truly know the ramifications of your retirement planning and where your money will be when you need it most. But understanding the whole truth about your money is worth the effort. It's the crucial initial step to creating your life's second act, rewarded by the time and energy invested in your life's first act.

LIVE AND SHARE
WITH PASSION

"When you retire, think and act as if you were still working; when you're still working, think and act a bit as if you were already retired."

—*Unknown*

As I said at this book's outset, life is long. And it is winding. There are many peaks to conquer and many valleys to cross. Too many times we wait until it is too late to really live and share with passion.

Too often, people and families let long periods of time go by where life is merely happening to them. With myriad obligations, it's easy to do, but it can lead to a sense of "Where does the time go?" and "Why don't I ever get to do what I want?"

I'm certainly not suggesting that you should wait until retirement to do what you want. But if time has gone by, and you feel like you never really got the chance to spend it as you'd like, retirement is a great time to strike out down that path. The Prosperity Economics Movement wants you to have the inspired drive, excellent health, and ample financial resources to explore your passions, examine your innate calling, and pursue your instinctive life—at any stage in life, but most deservedly at retirement.

So, with that said, below are a few suggestions to help you zero in on the possibilities that await:

- Make a "bucket list"—a list of fun things that you've always had a hankering to try, but haven't yet had the chance. (Check out the 2007 movie *The Bucket List* for some laughs and ideas.)

- Be sure to include some challenges on your bucket list. Your muscles and brain live in a "use it or lose it" environment, so every year pick one new thing to learn—all the better if a friend or your significant other can join you. Marriage-Builders.com has a great "Recreational Enjoyment Inventory" questionnaire to help you with this effort.

- Human beings were created to push limits, so push yourself a bit each week—for example, mentally, by doing something you aren't comfortable with; physically, by doubling your workout for a day; emotionally, by reaching out to someone whom you wouldn't have otherwise; and/or spiritually, by doubling your prayer or meditation time.

- Consider the concept of **both**—rather than either/or. How often do we humans think "A" *or* "B" instead of "A" *and* "B"? Consider adopting the idea of trying to get both. Strategize the various things you want to do or items you'd like to have and see if you can pull them both off. This will keep you thinking, and keep you excited and upbeat. When you are excited, others feel that excitement and catch it.

- Concentrate on what you can add to your health, rather than what you should give up. Add walking, water, or weights to your physical self care rather than focusing on trying to "lose weight" or "stop drinking coffee." The positive attention is more inspiring, and you'll get better results.

As I always aspire to practice what I preach, here's a list of positive changes I'm working on:

More:	Less:
Books	Magazines
Movies	TV
Water	Soda
Tea	Coffee
Veggies	Chips
Love	Resentment
Walking	Sitting
Saving	Spending
Recreation	Shopping
Gratitude	Complaining
Humility	Ego
Flow	Resistance

"The biggest motivation I have to keep competing
is that I feel I am improving."
~ *Japanese equestrian Hiroshi Hoketsu, the oldest Olympian,
at age 71, in London 2012. He competed first in the Tokyo Games
in 1964, then 44 years later in Beijing, and most recently in London
where he placed 17th in the individual dressage event.*

Top Ten Tips for Staying Young Physically

It is true that health is the foundation for wealth, and I encourage you to commit yourself to practicing habits that will keep you youthful at every age. Follow these tips from personal trainer Nancy Reidmann McVeigh, and you'll be able to live and share with passion into your 80s, 90s, and beyond:

1. Get a good night's sleep.
2. Stretch—it keeps the body limber and decreases your chance of injury.

3. Drink lots of water.
4. Eat a nutritious breakfast that includes protein and carbo-hydrates.
5. Eat high-fiber foods and limit foods high in saturated fat and sugar.
6. Have good posture—don't slouch.
7. Set goals to keep learning and growing.
8. Be physically active each day, doing something you enjoy.
9. Smile and be happy—it can be contagious.
10. Learn how to manage stress in healthy ways.

Life is an *and*. Life is not an *either/or*. Life is love *and* money. It is passion, purpose, finding your innate calling, *and* financial stability and physical security—especially if we are to appreciate this relatively peaceful and abundant time in history. I would like these things for you throughout your entire life, *and* I would like them for you at retirement.

To that end, here is a brief guide on moving through every stage in life with abundance and passion:

Age 20–35

For those of you early in your careers, keep seeking work you love so you can do that work for as long as possible. And get in the habit of saving 20 percent of your earnings, a habit that will pay off in droves in ways you have not yet conceived.

Age 35–55

For those of you in mid-life, if you haven't already begun saving, start now! There's no time like the present, and that effort can still pay off in spades when you least expect it. And, if you don't love your work, find other work—because you will want to be doing that work for many more years. In the meantime, allocate a portion of your savings to take long weekends, vacations, and even sabbaticals along the way.

Age 55 and up

For those of you near typical retirement age or past it, take some vacations, long weekends, and be well rested—so you can envision working for a longer period in your life than you had originally thought. For those of you already retired and loving it, keep doing what you're doing!

And for those retired and not loving it, find a way to provide value—this is what will get you excited again! It may take a few starts and stops until you find "your thing," but it will be well worth it—for yourself and for others.

$$* * * * *$$

The cultural portals of irrelevance, decline, and inertia at retirement are manufactured paradigms. The wisdom, discernment, and experience that come with age bring their own power, force, and beauty. Don't let our narcissistic, youth-obsessed, media-drenched culture influence your experience of your later years. Bring all the precious hard-earned attributes attained through life to bear on your later years and, subsequently, on society as a whole.

Each of you—each of us—still has much to give, and much to learn. As life expectancies increase worldwide, we now have more time in which to learn all of life's glorious lessons and scale the myriad Prosperity Peaks before us—now and long into our bold, uncharted future.

Retirement Profile: Sir John Marks Templeton (1912–2008)
Financier and Philanthropist
"Busting the Retirement Lies"

American-born Sir John Marks Templeton was founder of one of the most successful private financial services companies in the world. Templeton had a tendency to go against the flow. According to a July 27, 2008 article in *The Economist*, "In September 1939, when the war-spooked world was selling, he borrowed $10,000 to buy 100 shares in everything that was trading for less than a dollar a share on the New York Stock Exchange. All but four eventually turned profits. In early 2000, conversely, he sold all his dot-com and NASDAQ tech stocks just before the market crashed. His iron principle of investing was 'to buy when others are despondently selling and to sell when others are greedily buying.' At the point of 'maximum pessimism' he would enter, and clean up."

Despite Templeton's wild success in the market, his enthusiasm for life was never confined to the financial world nor was it limited to his younger years.

In 1973, at age 61, he started the Templeton Prize for Progress in Religion, an annual award given for individual achievement in "life's spiritual dimension," a dimension he felt had been disregarded for too long. In 1987, at the age of 75, he set up the Templeton Foundation to foster thoughtful inquiry into the subject of God and religious and spiritual life.

However, Templeton's Prize and Foundation were not the extent of his charitable giving. In *The Daily Telegraph*, his obituary exclaimed:

> … this was only a drop in the ocean of Templeton's philanthropy. He endowed university courses in spirituality and science, funded medical schools to run classes on healing and spirituality, and rewarded universities and individuals that upheld 'traditional educational values,' schools that promoted 'character development,' and colleges that taught market economics.

The *Economist* article, meanwhile, discussed some of Templeton's motivations, giving us insight into his philosophy:

> 'You can give away too much land and too much money,' said Sir John, 'but never enough love, and the real return was immediate: more love.' The Institute for Research on Unlimited Love, founded with his money, was set up to study this dynamic of the spiritual marketplace.

Over a decade after the institute's start, it is going strong and making a significant difference.

Sir Templeton never retired, even into his 90s. Every day, he took power walks against the ocean current by his Bermuda home, kept up with the markets for his charitable causes, and pondered questions about man's spiritual nature.

Immensely wealthy and going strong for decades past typical retirement age, Templeton shattered the retirement lies that plague us all. The philanthropist never stopped working and continued contributing, producing value, and enjoying that productivity his entire life.

CONCLUSION

To bring this book to a close, let's have a look at one more inspirational story—our final retirement profile—that prompts the question "What is the measure of a successful life?" After all, this is truly what retirement can answer; you've enjoyed a successful life that you can build upon, or your later years can serve as a time to accomplish those meaningful things you hadn't as a younger person. While no one person has all the answers, we feel Mr. Riedmann certainly gives us plenty to think about.

Retirement Profile: Arthur C. Riedmann (1921–)
"A Personal Account"

There are usually a number of factors involved when someone decides to keep working after reaching the age of 65. Those particular to me were:

1. My dear wife (of 57 years) and I had decided before marriage that we would like to have a large family. We were blessed with an answer to our prayers, and our family now includes four sons and five daughters. When I reached age 65, our home was still active with the presence of three of our children, as they continued with their high school and university educations.

2. My parents were German immigrants, with the work ethic of that nation,

and it was passed on to me—my father didn't retire until age 72. I also liked my job, which consisted of affording commercial property and liability coverages to major clients. The work was interesting and challenging, and with my professional degree in that industry, it was a good fit. This work ethic was also passed on to my only sibling—my brother, who became a Franciscan priest and continued some of his priestly duties until age 90. Now 96, he is in a clerical home for the aged in New Jersey.

3. My third consideration was financial. The insurance business is steady and afforded us the opportunity to always have a nice, clean, and happy home. At the same time, raising a family of nine did not permit much attention to retirement plans, nor were they typical in the industry in those days. So my period from age 65 to retirement at age 76 gave me an opportunity to finally pay more attention to that subject.

Goals for retirement

Prior to retirement, I had joined the St. Vincent de Paul Society and delivered food boxes to the needy on Saturdays. After retirement, I intended to stay active, and volunteering was my solution. My wife and were able to work weekdays delivering food boxes. Osborn School District began the Oasis program, which consisted of people my age helping children to improve their reading skills, and I was an original member of the program. I also joined Ozanam Manor, a transitional housing shelter for the homeless, as an interviewer and subsequently a mentor. We assisted our clients for up to six months, ultimately helping them return to society. Another enjoyable volunteering activity was ushering in Symphony Hall downtown Phoenix. But sorry to say, age does take its toll, so my sole volunteering activity now is the weekly watering of the front of our building (one of six) that composes our condominium community.

Staying physically active

My entire childhood in Brooklyn seemed to consist of sports activities. There were always enough children available on our street to start a game, and we played whatever was appropriate to the season: mostly hockey on roller skates, but also basketball and softball. There has never been a time in my life to vegetate—even now, my wife and I swim each day in our condominium pool, usually from April until the end of September. During the other six months of the year, we take daily walks. And tending to our rose garden and incidental activities satisfactorily fills the rest of the days.

I believe the above would indicate a successful life to the reader. It would be missing the fact that a spiritual outlook was the glue that held all this together. My wife and I attend Mass almost daily and thank God always for his blessings. The result is happiness—which we wish for all, especially for our family and anyone reading this attempt at retirement wisdom.

What is the measure of a successful retirement, or more importantly, a successful *life*? Of course, one must have the resources to do the things that are important to them—but "retirement" is about more than money, and a successful life is more than the ability to cease from one's work, if that is even desirable at all.

We think that Mr. Riedmann got it right. He designed a life that resulted in his own happiness, through spending time doing the things he loved and with those dearest to him. What kind of life will bring you the greatest happiness? We sincerely hope that this book will lead you to discover that for yourself. May your life be filled with peace, love, and every kind of prosperity. And do keep in touch with us—we'd love to hear *your* retirement stories about how you busted past the "typical" ideas of retirement to create a life of purpose, passion, and abundance!

Resources

Books

Don't Retire, REWIRE!
Jeri Sedlar and Rick Miners, ALPHA, second edition, 2007

LIFE Expectancy: It's Never Too Late to Change Your Game
William Keiper, FirstGlobal Partners LLC, 2012

The Ultimate Gift
Jim Stovall, David C. Cook (Publisher), 2007

Wealth Warrior: The Personal Prosperity Revolution
Steve Chandler, Maurice Bassett (Publisher), 2012

God Wants You to Be Rich
Paul Zane Pilzer, Simon and Schuster, 1995

Growing Old Is Not for Sissies (1 & 2)
Etta Clark, Pomegranate Publishers, 1986

Younger Next Year: Live Strong, Fit, and Sexy—Until You're 80 and Beyond
Dr. Henry Lodge and Chris Crowley, Workman Publishing, 2007

Busting the Financial Planning Lies: Learn to Use Prosperity Economics to Build Sustainable Wealth, Prosperity Economics Movement, 2012

Personal & Professional Development Websites

www.100Wisdom.com

www.Kolbe.com

www.InstinctiveLife.com

www.StrategicCoach.com

www.StrengthsFinder.com

Financial Education and Resources Websites

www.TruthConcepts.com

www.Partners4Prosperity.com

www.ProsperityPeaks.com

Networking and Volunteering Websites

www.NetworkForGood.org
Helps people connect with a cause

www.VolunteerMatch.org
Matches you to volunteer opportunities

www.PartnersInCare.org
Volunteer seniors use their time and talents to help others and, in exchange, receive help when they need it (only available in Maryland)

www.SeniorsHelpingSeniors.com
Seniors providing other seniors with in-home companionship, light housekeeping, cooking, gardening, transportation, and more

Work, Business, and Technology Websites

www.PivotPlanet.com
Looking for a new vocation? Connect with advisors in your field.

www.Freelance.com
Freelance work opportunities

www.RetiredBrains.com
Resources for seniors, including work and business opportunities

www.Seniors4Hire.org
Helping older workers find jobs

www.SeniorNet.org
Membership site for computer technology and Internet training

www.SeniorsGuideToComputers.com
Free resource site for computer training

www.SeniorJobBank.com
Connecting employers with qualified older workers for over a decade

Additional Online Information
http://rss.csmonitor.com/~r/feeds/csm/~3/ourlkr2To2c/
Why-we-work-and-keep-working

http://www.csmonitor.com/USA/Society/2012/0902/
The-silver-collar-economy

http://www.csmonitor.com/World/Asia-Pacific/2012/0902/
In-Japan-better-with-age

Films
The Ultimate Gift (based on the book by Jim Stovall)
Directed by Michael O. Sajbel, 2006

The Best Exotic Marigold Hotel
Directed by John Madden, 2011

Ghost Town
Directed by David Koepp, 2008

Notes

1. Eddy, Mary Baker. *Science and Health with Key to The Scriptures*. Boston: The Christian Science Board of Directors, 1875. Print.

2. Morganroth Gullette, Margaret. Interview by Julia M. Klein. "Interview With Margaret Morganroth Gullette on the New Ageism: Agewise calls for reexamination of negative views." *AARP Bulletin*, 31 Mar. 2011. Web. 26 Nov. 2013.

3. Durrett, Chuck. "Musings: Seniors versus Elders." *CoHousing*. The CoHousing Association of the United States, 1 Oct. 2008. Web. 26 Nov. 2013.

4. Wang H, Schumacher AE, Levitz CE, Mokdad AH, Murray CJL. "Left behind: widening disparities for males and females in US county life expectancy, 1985-2010." *Population Health Metrics*. 2013; 11:8.

5. Fletcher, Michael A. "Research ties economic inequality to gap in life expectancy." *Washington Post*, 10 Mar. 2013: Web. 26 Nov. 2013.

6. MelP. "Time to Retire the Concept of Retirement." *The Next Hill*, 13 Oct. 2009. Web. 30 Oct. 2013.

7,8. Veres, Bob. "A Trillion Here, A Trillion There…" *Inside Information*, July 2012: 6-10.

9. www.bls.gov/cpi/home.htm

Acknowledgments

"Give First." That is the title of a speech I wrote my senior year in college after being elected by my classmates to provide a Baccalaureate speech. The books I write are my attempt at giving first, and yet so many people gave to me, I find everything has gone full circle.

Anytime you share an idea with someone you are giving first, and so there are many people I'd like to thank for their ideas, their thinking, and their giving. This list is in no particular order and I have tried to say why I was thanking each person so that those of you who don't recognize names can still get meaning from this page. To those of you who do recognize a name (yours or someone else's), I smile back at you since I know seeing a recognized name in "lights" always brings a smile. Please also know I'm sure I've forgotten someone and for that I'm very sorry, as so many people do give first.

Todd Langford, my ever-supportive husband and creator of TruthConcepts.com software.

Robby Butler, kid #1, who just gave his own senior speech with diplomacy and grace.

Kaylea Butler, kid #2, whose level-headed and fun approach to life are an inspiration.

Everyone who contributed profiles in the book, because stories say so much.

The P4P team of Theresa Sheridan, Jill Molitor, Carrie Putman, Gabe Mendoza, and Dolores Zuniga who make work so enjoyable.

Kate Phillips, our marketing coach who makes us look good and has such a steady stream of great ideas, plus the ability to get them done.

Andrew Chapman, publishing advisor and service-provider, and Mona Kuljurgis, writer and editor, who've made the book look good and read even better.

Armin Sethna, who helped me write the first version.

Jim Kindred and Joe Marron who proofread early versions and made great suggestions.

My parents, Dan and Melissa Hays, who are excellent examples of "keep working."

Todd's parents, Phil and Carman Langford, who read early versions and made great suggestions.

Nancy Riedmann, my personal trainer who listens to me jabber for 60 minutes three times a week while we work out via phone and webcam. (Yes, really.)

Dan Sullivan and Babs Smith, whose Strategic Coach program has been a guiding light for me since 1995.

Todd Strobel, Chris Anderson, and Ryan Bradshaw, who are helping with the Prosperity Economics Movement.

My sister, Tammi Brannan, owner of InstinctiveLife.com and my best friend.

And of course, the many advisors nationwide who practice Prosperity Economics.

About the Author

Kim D. H. Butler is a leader in the Prosperity Economics Movement, and an often-interviewed expert on whole life insurance and alternative investments. She has also authored *Busting the Financial Planning Lies*, which explores the difference between "typical" financial planning and strategies used by the wealthy to create prosperity, and *Live Your Life Insurance*, a handbook for building wealth with whole life insurance.

Kim got her start in banking and then worked as a financial planner, obtaining her Series 7 and Series 65 licenses, and her CFP® designation. But she grew disillusioned over time, realizing that the practices of typical financial planning were irrelevant, misleading, and even harmful! The projections and assumptions of typical financial planning gave clients a false sense of security, but no guaranteed results. Recommended strategies subjected money to more future taxes, and put it under the use and control of others. Worst of all, the system *rewarded* planners when they convinced clients to put (and keep) their money at risk.

Driven to find a better way, Kim studied the commonalities

between wealth builders. She observed what worked and what didn't work in the real world, and found synergy between strategies that followed certain principles. These common principles later became the 7 Principles of Prosperity, a foundation of the Prosperity Economics Movement.

In 1999, Kim left her established company and created Partners for Prosperity, Inc., dedicated to the principles of Prosperity Economics. Rather than seeking "assets under management," the firm shows people how to build sustainable wealth by controlling and benefiting from their *own* assets. Partners for Prosperity, Inc. is a federally Registered Investment Advisory Firm that serves clients in all 50 states and publishes a blog as well as the *Prosperity on Purpose* online newsletter. Butler also publishes ProsperityPeaks.com, an education-based website for Prosperity Economics principles and strategies.

Kim's work as a non-traditional financial advisor has been recommended by financial thought leaders and authors such as Robert Kiyosaki (*Rich Dad, Poor Dad*), Tom Dyson, publisher of the *Palm Beach Letter* investment newsletter, Tom Wheelright (*Tax Free Wealth*), and Garret Gunderson (*Killing Sacred Cows*). She has been interviewed by Robert Kiyosaki, consulted by the *Palm Beach Letter* about "Income for Life" strategies, has appeared on the popular *Real Estate Guys* radio show, and is a frequent guest on Guide to Financial Peace radio.

Mona Kuljurgis is a writer and editor living near Washington, D.C. She thanks Kim Butler for revealing to her, via this and other projects, the whole truth about her money.

About the Prosperity Economics Movement

Before the rise of qualified retirement plans, the ever-present 401(k), and the financial planning industry, people built wealth with diligence and common-sense strategies. Investors created wealth through building equity and ownership in properties, businesses, and participating (dividend-paying) whole life insurance. Only a few dabbled in Wall Street stocks, or built "portfolios" on paper.

Wealthy people, in fact, have never stopped practicing what we call "Prosperity Economics."

Today, the common investor is steered away from traditional wealth-building methods. Instead, they are confronted with a confusing labyrinth of funds, rates and complex financial instruments of questionable value. Mutual funds have become so complex that even the people who sell them can't explain them, nor predict when investors are about to lose money. Worse yet, over 30 percent of the average investor's wealth is drained away in fees to a financial industry rife with conflicts of interest.

The Prosperity Economics Movement (P.E.M.) is a rediscovery of the traditional simple and trusted ways to grow and protect your money. It was started to provide American investors an alternative to "typical" financial planning, showing us how to control our own wealth instead of delegating our financial futures to corporations and the government.

In Prosperity Economics, wealth isn't measured by how much money you have, but by how much *freedom* you have with your money. The focus is on cash flow rather than net worth. Liquidity, control, and safety are valued over uncertain hopes of a high rate of return. (See the diagram on the next page for some key differences between Prosperity Economics and "typical" financial planning.)

The Prosperity Economics Movement is actually comprised of smaller movements that represent alternatives to a financial planning industry we believe has gone off course. You may have heard of The Infinite Banking Concept, Private or Family Banking, Rich Dad Strategies, Circle of Wealth, or Bank on Yourself. Advisors and agents within the movement may use different language and even suggest different financial strategies, but they honor a common set of principles, such as the 7 Principles of Prosperity articulated by Kim Butler.

Typical financial planning is better than nothing, and will get you partway up the hill, but we want to show you how to reach the "peaks" of prosperity. Prosperity Economics shows you how to grow your wealth safely and reliably, with maximum financial flexibility and cash flow. To find out more about Prosperity Economics and the P.E.M., we invite you to explore our website at ProsperityPeaks.com.

Financial Planning versus	**Prosperity Economics**™
Meets needs and goals only	Pursues wants and dreams
Minimizes requirements	Optimizes opportunities
Product oriented (only what you buy)	Strategy oriented (what you do)
Rate of return focused	Opportunity cost recovery focused
Institutions control your money	You control your money
Micro (vacuum) based	Macro (big picture) based
Net worth is measurement	Cash flow is measurement
Retirement oriented	Abundant/Freedom oriented
Lives only on interest	Spends and replaces principle
Money stays still	Money moves
Dollars do only one job	Dollars do many jobs

Work with a Prosperity Economics Advisor

If you don't like your cash sitting at 1 percent—taxable—and you want your investment to grow without the roller-coaster ride of the market, we can help. To explore alternative financial strategies that put you in the driver's seat, we invite you to have a no-cost, no-obligation conversation with a Prosperity Economics Advisor. Simply email Welcome@ProsperityPeaks.com to set an appointment with Kim or one of her hand-picked advisors.

We will find out more about you and your situation, and evaluate how your money might work harder without subjecting it to risk, unnecessary taxation, and never-ending fees. We'll likely suggest proven alternative approaches to "financial planning as usual," and we can even refer you to a truly effective debt solution if needed. We have found these strategies through experience, and they have worked well for our clients.

The three main areas of interest for most people are: cash storage, asset growth, and income. We help clients implement alternative strategies for each of these desires. Our cash strategy grows cash many times faster than typical bank CD rates, while deferring taxes and offering other benefits. Our stock market alternative (especially effective for accredited investors) has an excellent track record with our clients and is not affected by stock market conditions, interest rates, or politics. We can even suggest alternatives to bonds or annuities for cash flow that offer more attractive rates without requiring a long-term surrender of assets.

Simply send an email to Welcome@ProsperityPeaks.com to get started or find out more.

In the meantime, we invite you to explore ProsperityPeaks.com, a website dedicated to Prosperity Economics. And as a special thank-you for purchasing this book, readers of *Busting the Retirement Lies* can go to ProsperityPeaks.com/permission and download our special 16-page report, "Permission to Spend: How To Spend Your Principle, Save a Fortune on Taxes, Increase Your Cash Flow... *and Never Run Out of Money!*"

Book a Prosperity Economics Speaker for Your Next Event!

For general audiences

Throughout the country, Prosperity Economics spokespersons are available to speak about the differences between typical financial planning and Prosperity Economics, along with related financial topics.

Are you looking for a particular subject area? Perhaps your audience would like to learn:

- Retirement plan realities—why qualified plans don't perform as illustrated
- How to save without the risks and roller coaster of the stock market
- Qualified plan alternatives that can significantly reduce future taxes
- The impact of inflation and the danger of retiring too soon
- Saving enough? Why most of us need to save more!
- Financial Planning versus Prosperity Economics

For advisors

Author **Kim Butler** and Truth Concepts founder **Todd Langford** are available to speak to advisors or agents about Prosperity Economics, including a Truth Concepts demo that uses calculators and tools to illustrate some of the distinctions of Prosperity Economics. (Truth Concepts is financial software built for advisors yet available to anyone, dedicated to telling the whole truth about money.)

This 2–3 hour presentation is a fascinating eye-opener about various financial philosophies and concepts, and how to talk about and illustrate various financial strategies with clients. Contact Kim@Partners4Prosperity.com for details.

Truth Training

Langford and Butler also conduct seminars several times a year for advisors (anyone is welcome) on using Truth Concepts software. Purchase of the software is not necessary, any advisor can benefit, and some find it so beneficial they return again and again! For more information, go to TruthConcepts.com.

The Prosperity Economics Movement is a not-for-profit organization comprising financial experts who practice Prosperity Economics and individuals who would like to learn how to apply the principles of Prosperity Economics to improve their lives. This book is part of a growing body of information that will support the organization and its members.

To learn more or buy your own copy of this book, go to:
www.ProsperityPeaks.com